GRADUATE RECORD EXAMINATION

PSYCHOLOGY

Advanced Test

James W. Morrison

ARCO PUBLISHING, INC.
219 PARK AVENUE SOUTH, NEW YORK, N.Y. 10003

Published by Arco Publishing, Inc.
219 Park Avenue South, New York, NY 10003

Library of Congress Cataloging in Publication Data

Arco Publishing Company, New York.
Graduate record examination, psychology advanced test.

1. Psychology—Study and teaching (Graduate)
2. Graduate record examination. I. Title.

BF78.A72 1979 150'.76 79-11444

ISBN 0-668-04762-3 (Paper Edition)

Printed in the United States of America

CONTENTS

PART ONE: WHAT YOU SHOULD KNOW ABOUT THE GRADUATE RECORD EXAMINATION ADVANCED TEST

PART TWO: SAMPLE GRE ADVANCED TESTS IN PSYCHOLOGY

Part I

What You Should Know About The Graduate Record Examination Advanced Test

THE ADVANCED PSYCHOLOGY TEST

The Purpose

The Advanced Psychology Test for the Graduate Record Examination is required by many graduate schools as part of their admissions selection program. Colleges may also use it to evaluate the achievements of their seniors who major in psychology. The test is administered by the Educational Testing Service of Princeton, New Jersey.

The Nature Of The Test

The test, which is two hours, 50 minutes long, is designed to probe broad understanding of the entire field of psychology rather than any specified area. It measures a student's knowledge of facts, concepts, principles, and theories, as well as his ability to evaluate and apply this knowledge appropriately.

The Advanced Test in Psychology consists of multiple-choice questions (approximately 200). Some of the stimulus materials, such as description of an experiment or graphs of psychological functions, serve as the basis for several questions and groups of optional responses. The questions come from undergraduate courses within the broadly defined field of psychology, i.e., to identify psychologists associated with particular theories or conclusions and to recall information from psychology courses. In addition, some questions require analyzing relationships, applying principles, drawing conclusions from experimental data, and evaluating experiments.

The questions in the Advanced Psychology Test usually include material covering the following areas:

1. General background information. This area is the source of the largest group of questions. It embraces the information a student should have acquired during his undergraduate studies in psychology, including historical and applied psychology.

2. Psychology of personality, including abnormal and clinical psychology.

3. Educational, child, social, industrial, and developmental psychology.

4. Psychodynamics, experimental methodology, statistics, physiology, motivation, perceptions, history of systems, and other sub-topics with which the college psychology major should have some familiarity.

The Advanced Test in Psychology produces two subscores in addition to the total score. The subscores help students identify their strengths and weaknesses and aid institutions in admissions and placement decisions. The test offers two subscores:

1. Experimental Psychology, with questions distributed about equally among learning, physiological and comparative, and perception and sensory psychology; and

2. Social Psychology, with questions distributed about equally among personality, clinical and abnormal, developmental, and social psychology.

Evidence from students' performance on test questions shows that questions within each of the two subscore categories are more closely related to each other than are questions in different categories. Each of the subscores reported for the Advanced Psychology Test is based on approximately 40 percent of the questions in the entire test.

The total score for the Advanced Psychology Test ranges from 760 to 320; the mean is 529 and the standard deviation is 94. The subscores range from 76 to 30; the mean 52.9 for Experimental Psychology (SD 9.4), and the mean of 53.1 for Social Psychology (SD 9.4). Graduate schools are provided with the statistical meaning of GRE scores and admissions committee interprets these scores according to the needs of its own programs.

OTHER ADVANCED TESTS

Advanced Tests are offered for the following subjects:

Biology
Chemistry
Computer Science
Economics
Education
Engineering
French
Geology
Government
History
Literature
Mathematics
Music
Philosophy
Physical Education
Physics
Psychology
Sociology
Spanish
Speech

Candidates may take only one of the Advanced Tests on one test date.

HOW QUESTIONS ARE TO BE ANSWERED

The following will help you become familiar with the way in which answers are to be recorded.

30. Chicago is a

A. state
B. city
C. country
D. town
E. village

Sample Answer Spaces:

30 A B C D E

Note that the letters of the suggested answers appear on the answer sheet and that you are to blacken the space beneath the letter of the answer you wish to give.

(You will record your answers on special answer sheets. Careful marking of the answer sheet is necessary so that it will be accurately graded by the test scoring machine.)

Applying For The Examination

Requests for information and application forms should be sent to:

The Graduate Record Examination
Educational Testing Service
Box 955
Princeton, New Jersey 08540

Every candidate is required to file a formal application and pay an examination fee.

You will be sent a ticket of admission giving the exact address of the place to which you should report for assignment to an examination room. Do not expect to receive your ticket until approximately one month before the examination date. You will be required to show your ticket to the supervisor at each session of the examinations. Normally, no candidate will be admitted to the examination room without his ticket of admission.

A candidate who loses his ticket should immediately write or wire the issuing office for a duplicate authorization. If in unusual circumstances a supervisor admits a candidate who does not have proper authorization, Educational Testing Service will review the case and will report the scores only if in its judgment the circumstances warranted the candidate's admission.

Rules For Conduct Of Examinations

No books, slide rules, compasses, rulers, dictionaries, or papers of any kind may be taken into the examination room; you are urged not to bring them to the center at all. Supervisors will not permit anyone found to have such materials with him to continue a test. Anyone giving or receiving any kind of assistance during a test will be asked to leave the room. His testbook and answer sheet will be taken from him and returned to ETS, the answer sheet will not be scored, and the incident will be reported to the institutions named to receive the score report.

Scratch work may be done in the margins of the testbooks. Scratch paper is not permitted.

You must turn in all testbooks and answer sheets at the close of the examination period. No test materials, documents, or memoranda of any sort are to be taken from the room. Disregard of this rule will be considered as serious an offense as cheating.

The examinations will be held only on the day and at the time scheduled. Be on time. Under no circumstances will supervisors honor requests for a change in schedule. You will not be permitted to continue a test or any part of it beyond the established time limit. You should bring a watch.

To avoid errors or delay in reporting scores:

1. Always use the same form of your name in signing your application form, your answer sheets, and on any correspondence with ETS. Do not write "John T. Jones, Sr." one time, and "J. T. Jones" another. Such inconsistency makes correct identification of papers difficult.

2. Write legibly at all times.

Transmitting The Results

You will receive a report of your scores directly from Educational Testing Service. You may also have your scores reported to as many as three graduate or professional schools without additional fee, provided you designate them in the appropriate place on your application. After registration closes, you may not substitute for or delete institutions already listed on your application. No partial reports will be issued; reports will include scores made on all tests taken on a given date. To avoid duplication of requests, you should keep a record of the institutions to which you have requested that scores be sent.

In designating on the application the institutions to which reports are to be sent, you should state the school, division, or department of the university or college as well as the name of the parent institution. Although arrangements have been made by most of the institutions for ETS to send all Advanced Test score reports to only one office at each institution, it may be necessary in some instances for ETS to know which school, division, or department has requested you to have your scores submitted.

Score reports requested on the application or by letter before the closing date will be issued within five weeks after your examination date. Although score reports requested after the closing date cannot be sent as quickly, they will be issued as soon as possible.

Scores on all Advanced Tests taken in the National Program for Graduate School Selection are available to any institution requesting them, whether or not the candidate himself has asked that a report be sent.

WHY USE THIS BOOK?

If you are planning to take the Graduate Record Examination Advanced Test, this book is indispensable for a higher score.

You are well aware that the GRE Advanced Test is one of the most important examinations that you will have ever taken. The results of this test will determine, in great measure, whether you will be admitted to the graduate school of your choice. Your entire future may well depend on the results of the GRE Advanced Test.

There will be many other candidates taking the test - and not all will score well enough to be accepted by the graduate schools of their choice. There simply are not enough places in the nation's better graduate schools to accommodate all applicants, worthy as they may be.

This book is designed to guide you in your study so that you will SCORE HIGH ON YOUR GRADUATE RECORD EXAMINATION ADVANCED TEST. This claim - that you will get a higher rating - has both educational and psychological validity for these reasons:

1. YOU WILL KNOW WHAT TO STUDY - A candidate will do better on a test if he knows what to study. The GRE-type questions in this book will tell you what to study.

2. YOU WILL SPOTLIGHT YOUR WEAKNESSES - In using this book, you will discover where your weaknesses lie. This self-diagnosis will provide you with a systematic procedure of study whereby you will spend your time where it will do you the most good.

3. YOU WILL GET THE "FEEL" OF THE EXAM - It is important to get the "feel" of the entire examination. Gestalt (meaning configuration or pattern) psychology stresses that true learning results in a grasp of the entire situation. Gestalists also tell us that we learn by "insight." One of the salient facets of this type of learning is that we succeed in "seeing through" a problem as a consequence of experiencing previous similar situations. This book contains hundreds and hundreds of "similar situations" - so you will discover when you take the actual examination.

4. YOU WILL GAIN CONFIDENCE - While preparing for the exam, you will build up confidence, and you will retain this confidence when you enter the exam room. This feeling of confidence will be a natural consequence of reason "3" above (getting the "feel" of the exam).

5. YOU WILL ADD TO YOUR KNOWLEDGE - "The learned become more learned." In going over the practice questions in this book, you will not - if you use this book properly -

be satisfied merely with the answer to a particular question. You will want to do additional research on the other choices of the same question. In this way, you will broaden your background to be adequately prepared for the exam to come, since it is quite possible that a question on the exam which you are going to take may require your knowing the meaning of one of these other choices. Thorndike's principle of "identical elements" explains this important phase of learning - particularly as it applies to examination preparation.

Part II

Advanced Tests in Psychology

AN ANALYSIS OF THE TEST

An analysis of recent GRE Advanced Tests in Psychology reveals the following:

1. Quite a number of questions deal with General Psychology. Every Psychology major is expected to be well-grounded in this phase.

2. The remaining questions take in

   a. Abnormal Psychology
   b. Clinical Psychology
   c. Social Psychology
   d. Educational Psychology
   e. Industrial Psychology
   f. Comparative Psychology
   g. Developmental Psychology
   h. Child Psychology

3. A topical classification of the GRE question types would embrace the following:

   (1) Learning Theory
   (2) Social Interaction
   (3) Psychodynamics
   (4) Experimental Methodology
   (5) History including Theories and Systems
   (6) Motivation
   (7) Perception
   (8) Sensory Processes
   (9) Growth
   (10) Physiology
   (11) Statistics
   (12) Tests

4. The questions are presented in two ways:

   A. Discrete questions
   B. Group questions - that is, a number of questions are based on a passage or a graph or a chart or a set of statistics. Usually two or three questions are in each set.

TEAR OUT ALONG THIS LINE AND MARK YOUR ANSWERS AS INSTRUCTED IN THE TEXT.

ANSWER SHEET TEST (1)

1 A B C D E
2 A B C D E
3 A B C D E
4 A B C D E
5 A B C D E
6 A B C D E
7 A B C D E
8 A B C D E
9 A B C D E
10 A B C D E
11 A B C D E
12 A B C D E
13 A B C D E
14 A B C D E
15 A B C D E
16 A B C D E
17 A B C D E
18 A B C D E
19 A B C D E
20 A B C D E
21 A B C D E
22 A B C D E
23 A B C D E
24 A B C D E
25 A B C D E
26 A B C D E
27 A B C D E
28 A B C D E
29 A B C D E
30 A B C D E
31 A B C D E
32 A B C D E
33 A B C D E
34 A B C D E
35 A B C D E
36 A B C D E
37 A B C D E
38 A B C D E
39 A B C D E
40 A B C D E
41 A B C D E
42 A B C D E
43 A B C D E
44 A B C D E
45 A B C D E
46 A B C D E
47 A B C D E
48 A B C D E
49 A B C D E
50 A B C D E
51 A B C D E
52 A B C D E
53 A B C D E
54 A B C D E
55 A B C D E
56 A B C D E
57 A B C D E
58 A B C D E
59 A B C D E
60 A B C D E
61 A B C D E
62 A B C D E
63 A B C D E
64 A B C D E
65 A B C D E
66 A B C D E
67 A B C D E
68 A B C D E
69 A B C D E
70 A B C D E
71 A B C D E
72 A B C D E
73 A B C D E
74 A B C D E
75 A B C D E
76 A B C D E
77 A B C D E
78 A B C D E
79 A B C D E
80 A B C D E
81 A B C D E
82 A B C D E
83 A B C D E
84 A B C D E
85 A B C D E
86 A B C D E
87 A B C D E
88 A B C D E
89 A B C D E
90 A B C D E
91 A B C D E
92 A B C D E
93 A B C D E
94 A B C D E
95 A B C D E
96 A B C D E
97 A B C D E
98 A B C D E
99 A B C D E
100 A B C D E
101 A B C D E
102 A B C D E
103 A B C D E
104 A B C D E
105 A B C D E
106 A B C D E
107 A B C D E
108 A B C D E
109 A B C D E
110 A B C D E
111 A B C D E
112 A B C D E
113 A B C D E
114 A B C D E
115 A B C D E
116 A B C D E
117 A B C D E
118 A B C D E
119 A B C D E
120 A B C D E
121 A B C D E
122 A B C D E
123 A B C D E
124 A B C D E
125 A B C D E
126 A B C D E
127 A B C D E
128 A B C D E
129 A B C D E
130 A B C D E
131 A B C D E
132 A B C D E
133 A B C D E
134 A B C D E
135 A B C D E
136 A B C D E
137 A B C D E
138 A B C D E
139 A B C D E
140 A B C D E
141 A B C D E
142 A B C D E
143 A B C D E
144 A B C D E
145 A B C D E
146 A B C D E
147 A B C D E
148 A B C D E
149 A B C D E
150 A B C D E
151 A B C D E
152 A B C D E
153 A B C D E
154 A B C D E
155 A B C D E
156 A B C D E
157 A B C D E
158 A B C D E
159 A B C D E
160 A B C D E
161 A B C D E
162 A B C D E
163 A B C D E
164 A B C D E
165 A B C D E
166 A B C D E
167 A B C D E
168 A B C D E
169 A B C D E
170 A B C D E
171 A B C D E
172 A B C D E
173 A B C D E
174 A B C D E
175 A B C D E
176 A B C D E
177 A B C D E
178 A B C D E
179 A B C D E
180 A B C D E
181 A B C D E
182 A B C D E
183 A B C D E
184 A B C D E
185 A B C D E
186 A B C D E
187 A B C D E
188 A B C D E
189 A B C D E
190 A B C D E
191 A B C D E
192 A B C D E
193 A B C D E
194 A B C D E
195 A B C D E
196 A B C D E
197 A B C D E
198 A B C D E
199 A B C D E
200 A B C D E

GRE ADVANCED TEST IN PSYCHOLOGY

SAMPLE TEST 1

Time: 2 hours and 50 minutes

Directions: Select from the lettered choices that choice which best completes the statement or answers the question. Write the letter of your choice on the answer sheet.

1. The blind spot or optic disk

   A. receives an image of a point, such as the vertex of an angle, when the point is located in the nasal half of the visual field of the eye
   B. is located in the fovea of the eye
   C. falls slightly above the horizontal retinal meridian
   D. has neither retinal rods nor cones since nerve fibers leave the eye at this point to form the optic nerve
   E. is located in the retina

2. In contrast to the rods

   A. almost every cone has a connection through a bipolar cell to an individual fiber of the optic nerve
   B. cones are very thinly distributed around the fovea
   C. cones are not in the retina
   D. cones are sensitive only to light from an incandescent light source
   E. cones are not connected with bipolar cells

3. Pitch is the psychological aspect of tonal sound determined principally by the physical dimension of

   A. intensity
   B. frequency
   C. waveform
   D. duty cycle
   E. none of the above

4. A student is asked to recite a poem he has previously memorized. His retention of the poem is being tested by the technique of

   A. savings
   B. recognition
   C. recall
   D. transfer
   E. repetition

5. According to E. C. Tolman, the primary effect of reinforcement is

   A. drive reduction
   B. need reduction
   C. tension reduction
   D. to change the stimulus situation
   E. to confirm the expectancy of the subject

6. Teaching machines are primarily a development of the work of

   A. J. A. Taylor
   B. C. L. Hull
   C. E. R. Guthrie
   D. E. C. Tolman
   E. B. F. Skinner

7. The mean of sample data is

A. equal to the mean of the population
B. equal to the mean of the universe
C. an estimate of the mean of the universe
D. equal to the median of the sample
E. equal to the mode of the sample

8. Moving toward, away from, and against people are personality descriptions found in the formulations of

A. H. S. Sullivan
B. Karen Horney
C. Henry Murray
D. Alfred Adler
E. Erich Fromm

9. According to Freud, moral anxiety

A. is aroused only when punishment is threatened by the real world
B. is experienced by the id as guilt or shame
C. is experienced by the ego as guilt or shame
D. is experienced by the superego as guilt or shame
E. is experienced by both ego and superego as guilt or shame

10. In a 1948 experiment investigating the effect of frustration on the play of children, Barker, Dembo, and Levin

A. found that in the frustrating situation most of the children actually increased the constructiveness of their play since they used the toys to alleviate the frustrating situation
B. concluded that in the frustrating situation, the constructiveness of the children's play was significantly reduced as compared to a control situation which was free from frustration
C. were unable to confirm a reduction in the constructiveness of the children's play due to frustration since the experimenters found they had manipulated too many variables
D. shocked the children mildly each time they attempted to play with highly attractive toys
E. used adrenalin to increase the children's emotionality

11. According to the trace theory of memory

A. the past is assumed to be represented in the present by a trace which persists from an earlier experience
B. a present process can reactivate a trace of a prior experience resulting in a new process of recall or recognition
C. both A and B are correct
D. neither A or B is correct
E. B is always correct; A is correct only in certain cultures

12. According to E. R. Guthrie, forgetting is the result of

A. decay of excitation
B. interference of new learning with old learning
C. disuse
D. both A and C
E. both B and C

13. According to C. Jung

A. not all people have a collective unconscious
B. although everyone has a collective unconscious, it has little bearing on what one learns from his experiences
C. the collective unconscious is the same as the racial unconscious
D. the collective unconscious cannot be inherited
E. the collective unconscious is much the same for all men

14. An example of an operational definition of "hunger" would be the experimenter's observation that

A. the animal wanted food
B. the animal was deprived of food for 24 hours prior to the experiment
C. the animal had a "hungry look"
D. none of the above is correct
E. the animal licked its lips repeatedly

15. Measurement scales which have a meaningful "0" point are called

A. nominal scales
B. interval scales
C. ratio scales
D. ordinal scales
E. non-parametric scales

16. Random assignment of a different number to each person in a group is an example of

A. an ordinal scale
B. a ratio scale
C. a nominal scale
D. an interval scale
E. a parametric scale

17. A few extreme scores in a distribution

A. will affect the value of the median more than that of the mean
B. will affect the value of the mean more than that of the median
C. will affect the values of the mean and the median equally
D. will affect neither the median nor the mean
E. will affect the value of the mode more than that of the mean

18. The eye is sensitive to wavelengths of electromagnetic radiation ranging from about

A. 600 to 1,000 millimicrons
B. 16 to 16,000 millimicrons
C. 100 to 500 millimicrons
D. 120 to 800 millimicrons
E. 400 to 700 millimicrons

19. The psychological method in which the threshold is determined by the stimulus value which is reported as detected by the subject 50% of the time, is

A. the method of limits or method of minimal changes
B. the method of adjustment
C. the method of constant stimuli
D. none of the above
E. the method of variable stimuli

20. The psychophysical method which is particularly subject to errors of anticipation and errors of habituation is

A. the method of constant stimuli
B. the method of limits
C. the method of constant stimulus difference
D. none of the above
E. the method of adjustment

21. The standard unit for signifying the luminous intensity of a point source of light is

A. a lumen
B. a foot-candle
C. candles per square meter
D. a radian
E. the International Candle

22. The illuminance falling on a surface is

A. inversely proportional to the square of the distance from the source to the surface
B. directly proportional to the square of the distance from the source to the surface
C. twice the square of the distance from the source to the surface
D. the cube root of the distance from the source to the surface
E. the natural logarithm of the square of the distance from the source to the surface

23. When light changes from dim to bright, the pupil of the eye

A. constricts
B. dilates
C. constricts or dilates depending on the individual
D. remains a constant area
E. becomes lighter

24. Additive mixing of light of the correct proportions of luminance of three wavelengths, one from the violet-blue, one from the green, and one from the red region of the spectrum, results in

A. grey
B. black
C. beige
D. brown
E. white

25. The scatter diagram is preferred by some statisticians to the coefficient of correlation. Which of the following statements are reasons for such preference?

I. The nature of the relationship can be determined by the scatter diagram.
II. The scatter diagram is not subject to the assumption of linearity.
III. The scatter diagram involves no mathematical computations.
IV. The coefficient of correlation can be determined without mathematical manipulations.
V. Multiple independent variables can be tested at one time.

A. I only
B. II only
C. III and IV only
D. IV and V only
E. I, II, and III only

26. It has been found that there is no chromatic sensation in

A. the most central portions of the retina
B. the temporal half of each retina
C. the nasal half of each retina
D. the most peripheral portions of the retina
E. the cornea

27. Helmholtz's concept of "unconscious inference" refers to

A. perception in the size-distance relationship
B. unconscious determination of emotions
C. rationalization
D. sublimation
E. displacement

28. The semantic differential technique of obtaining a quantified description of word-meaning was developed by

A. Hull
B. Skinner
C. Schachter
D. Keller and Schoenfeld
E. Osgood

29. Identify the name or designation which is not appropriately grouped with the others.

A. hysteria
B. amnesia
C. dissociative reaction
D. fugue
E. aphasia

30. Freud's first great published work dealing with psychoanalytic and personality theory was

A. Psychopathology of Everyday Life
B. The Interpretation of Dreams
C. Beyond the Pleasure Principle
D. Three Essays on Sexuality
E. Civilization and Its Discontents

31. The talking-out technique of treating hysteria was introduced to Freud by

A. Jean Charcot
B. Carl Jung
C. Joseph Breuer
D. Ernest Jones
E. Alfred Adler

32. According to Freud, everything psychological that is inherited and that is present at the time of birth is contained in the

A. id and superego
B. id and ego
C. superego
D. ego
E. id

33. The id derives its psychic energy from

    A. outer reality
    B. the bodily processes
    C. from the ego
    D. from conflicts
    E. from the superego

34. When increases in tension are experienced by the id as uncomfortable states of tension, the id

    A. functions to discharge the tension immediately
    B. becomes helpless
    C. regresses
    D. postpones the discharge of tension until such time as the discharge will be realistically possible
    E. cannot function

35. An example of the primary process in normal people is

    A. reflex action
    B. reality testing
    C. reaction formation
    D. introjection
    E. the nocturnal dream

36. Wish fulfillment is an example of

    A. reflex action
    B. the primary process
    C. the reality principle
    D. the secondary process
    E. introjection

37. The status of a population in terms of a characteristic under investigation in a psychological study is most often described by the

    A. mean of the observations
    B. median of the observations
    C. mode of the observations
    D. standard deviation of the observations
    E. analysis of variance

38. The id, in contract to the ego

    A. knows wish-fulfilling mental images and the outer world
    B. knows only the outer world
    C. transacts between the organism and the outer world
    D. knows only wish-fulfilling mental images
    E. can censor the superego

39. Identify the name or designation which is not appropriately grouped with the others.

    A. deuteranopia
    B. protanopia
    C. presbyopia
    D. tritanopia
    E. color blindness

40. The reality principle operates by means of the secondary process to

    A. serve ultimately the pleasure principle
    B. suspend temporarily the pleasure principle
    C. prevent tension discharge until an object satisfying the need has been discovered
    D. do all of the above
    E. do both A and C

41. The ego derives its energy

    A. directly from the body process
    B. from the superego
    C. from no source other than itself
    D. from the id
    E. from both id and superego

42. The portion of the superego which punishes is

    A. the libido
    B. the ego-ideal
    C. the whole superego
    D. all of the above
    E. the conscience

43. The absolute threshold curves of rod and cone vision, plotted as a function of wavelength, indicate that

    A. above 700 millimicrons, the cones are more sensitive than the rods
    B. below 600 millimicrons, the cones are more sensitive than the rods

C. below 600 millimicrons the rods are more sensitive than the cones
D. both A and C are correct
E. both B and C are correct

44. A statistical test which indicates the chance or probability of an observed or greater difference between two means occurring by chance is called a test of

A. significance
B. means
C. ratios
D. normalcy
E. none of the above

45. When a person fixates a point in space, the area of the eye on which the point falls is the

A. optic disc
B. fovea
C. visual angle
D. blindspot
E. optic chiasma

46. The rods and cones of the eye are located

A. in the pupil
B. in the optic nerve
C. toward the back of the retina
D. in the ciliary body
E. in the iris

47. It has been found that, especially in the foveal region, the acuity provided by the cones

A. is greater than the acuity provided by the rods
B. is less than the acuity provided by the rods
C. is equal to the acuity provided by the rods
D. cannot be determined
E. has less intensity than the acuity provided by the rods

48. In experimental studies of simple reaction time using optimal stimulus values, it has been the general finding that

A. reaction time to a visual stimulus is shorter than reaction time to an auditory stimulus
B. reaction time to an auditory stimulus is shorter than reaction time to a visual stimulus
C. there is no difference in reaction time to visual and auditory stimuli
D. reaction time to auditory stimuli has not been determined
E. reaction time to visual stimuli depends solely on the intensity of the stimuli

49. If the arithmetic mean of a distribution is 160, the mode 161, and the median 163--then the mean of the standard normal curve would be

A. 0
B. 8
C. 8.1
D. 5200
E. 161

50. Experimental findings in maze learning seem to show that

A. errors are eliminated most quickly from the middle of a maze
B. errors are eliminated most quickly from the beginning and end of the maze
C. there is no difference among beginning, middle, and end of a maze with regard to elimination of error
D. there are no consistent findings, with regard to elimination of error, in maze learning experiments
E. no serial position effect exists in maze learning

51. Retroactive inhibition refers to

A. improvement in performance of a task over a period of no practice
B. improvement in performance of a task as a result of practice on a previous task
C. interference with retention of a task because of subsequent activity
D. the savings method of retention
E. the recall method of retention

52. Usually it has been found that verbal and motor <u>retention</u> curves, plotted

as a function of time between original learning and testing, are

A. positively accelerated increasing curves
B. positively accelerated decreasing curves
C. negatively accelerated increasing curves
D. negatively accelerated decreasing curves
E. directly accelerated increasing curves

53. When the standard deviation of a population is estimated from sample data and the sample is relatively small, the distribution to be used is

A. the normal distribution
B. the "t" distribution
C. the chi-squared distribution
D. the "F" distribution
E. the hypergeometric distribution

54. In the measurement of retention, the general finding has been that after any given interval

A. recognition scores are better than recall scores
B. recall scores are better than recognition scores
C. there is no difference between recall and recognition retention scores
D. none of the foregoing types of comparisons is ever made
E. there is no difference between savings and recall scores

55. The first recognized psychological laboratory was established at Leipzig in 1879 by

A. E. B. Titchener
B. E. L. Thorndike
C. H. Ebbinghaus
D. E. Mach
E. W. Wundt

56. Karl S. Lashley, as a result of his 1920 and 1930 experiments involving the cortex of the brain of rats and other animals, found that

A. there were separate areas in the brain for each learned task
B. when part of the cortex is removed, a rat cannot relearn a maze
C. the greater the amount of cortex removed from the brain of the rat, the more difficult learning seemed to be
D. a theory of point-to-point connection in a reflex chain best explained brain activity
E. decortication does not affect maze learning ability

57. J. B. Watson is famous for having described thinking in terms of

A. central neural process
B. implicit speech movements
C. memory images
D. unconscious mental actions
E. sensations and images

58. According to McDougall,

A. propensities directly motivate adult human behavior
B. there are only two major human propensities
C. all human behavior is instinctive
D. there are only two major human sentiments
E. sentiments derived from propensities, and still possessing their emotional striving, motivate adult human behavior

59. A test which has a reliability coefficient of .25 cannot have a validity coefficient between the test and the independent criterion to which it is predicting, greater than

A. .05
B. .50
C. .25
D. .025
E. .005

60. In the 1960 revision of the Stanford-Binet, the IQ of a subject is computed

A. by dividing his MA obtained on the test by his CA

B. by dividing his MA obtained on the test by his CA, and multiplying the result by 100
C. by comparing his MA obtained on the test with prepared tables which give an IQ based on the standard deviations of MA's for a representative sample of persons at each age
D. by multiplying his MA obtained in the test by the standard deviation for that MA, and dividing the result by his CA; then multiplying the latter result by 100
E. by dividing CA by MA

61. Terman and Oden (1947), in their study investigating high IQ children through adulthood, found

A. that, as adults, these people were markedly inferior physically to average people of the same age
B. that, as adults, these people were superior in most ways to average adults of the same age
C. that, as adults, these people were equal in most ways to average adults of the same age
D. that a surprisingly small number of them entered college
E. that a surprisingly high percentage became skilled laborers

62. In the T-score system of derived scores,

A. the mean is set at 100 and the standard deviation at 10
B. the mean is set at 0 and the standard deviation at .5
C. the mean is set at 75 and the standard deviation at 16
D. the mean is set at 50 and the standard deviation at 10
E. the mean is set at 0 and the standard deviation at 10

63. A raw score of 25 (mean = 20, standard deviation = 4) could be converted into a z-score of

A. +1.25 B. -1.25
C. -5 D. +12.5
E. +5

64. When observations form a "normal" distribution about their mean, approximately what percent of the observations fall within one standard deviation above and one standard deviation below the mean?

A. 50 percent
B. 95 percent
C. 33 percent
D. 67 percent
E. 75 percent

65. The crucial sympton is a determination of whether to apply the label neurosis or psychosis is most likely to be

A. fixation
B. sexual preoccupation
C. anxiety
D. obsessive thinking
E. hallucinations

66. The phobic person is different from the paranoic in that the phobic

A. does not utilize symbolism in his disorder
B. does not cognitively believe in the objective danger to which his anxiety is attached
C. does not displace the object of his temptation or fear
D. does not project his emotions onto an object
E. does not introject

67. In Freud's theory of the "anal" characteristics of obsessive neuroses, obstinacy is described as

A. a reaction formation
B. an atoning ritual
C. an elaboration of early submission
D. an elaboration of early rebellion
E. a fixation

68. The statement, "The important thing in the field of psychometrics is to view the result of every test in the light of the degree of its probability," means that, from the standpoint of statistics,

A. the mathematical probability of having a given event or events occur is the primary basis of evaluating test results
B. the probability that study samples are representative of the population is the primary basis of evaluating test results
C. high probability that chance can explain observed study differences is the basis for determing that the differences are significant
D. B and C above
E. none of the above

69. Guthrie and Horton concluded from their experiments with cats in a puzzle-box that

A. the best prediction of what an animal will do is based on what he does in the majority of similar situations
B. no conclusions on general learning theory can be drawn from experiments with cats
C. the prediction of what an animal will do at a particular time is best made on the basis of what the animal has been observed to do last in the same situation
D. the most important finding about their cat's behavior was the variety of activities observed
E. cats never show stereotyped behavior

70. In the 1942 experiment of Seward, comparing acquisition of a bar-pressing response rewarded by food with acquisition of the same response when the animal is removed from the cage after pressing the bar,

A. Guthrie might have explained the finding that the response was more readily acquired with a food reward by maintaining that the reward effected more complete removal from the stimulus situation than did the actual removal
B. Seward felt his results supported Guthrie's theoretical position in regard to reinforcement
C. the animals learned the response more readily when they were removed from the situation
D. either B or C is correct
E. the results confirmed Tohnan's theories

71. The deviations of actual data from a regression line are

A. a maximum
B. zero
C. always greater than zero
D. always negative
E. always infinity

72. The normal prototype of obsessional neuroses is found in

A. free association
B. reaction formation
C. flight from objective danger
D. transient hallucinations resulting from fatigue
E. logical thinking

73. According to Skinner, a negative reinforcer is defined as being

A. the same as punishment
B. a stimulus whose removal strengthens an operant
C. a stimulus whose presence depresses responses
D. a noxious stimulus
E. both C and D

74. In the 1953 experiment of Kimball and Kendal comparing extinction by the toleration method with extinction by the usual exhaustion method, the experimenters concluded

A. that the results, with the exhaustion procedure resulting in more rapid extinction, supported Hull's theory of extinction
B. that the results, with the toleration method giving more rapid extinction, supported Guthrie's theoretical explanations of extinction
C. that the results, with the exhaustion procedure resulting in more rapid extinction, supported Guthrie's theory of extinction
D. that the results, with the toleration method giving more rapid extinction, supported Hull's theoretical explanations of extinction

E. there was no difference in extinction produced by toleration or by exhaustion

75. Guthrie explains that punishment is most successful in changing behavior

A. when the response that brings on punishment is incompatible with the last response to the punished situation
B. when punishment produces an emotional response in both the person administering the punishment and the one receiving it
C. when the response that brings on punishment is compatible with the last response to the punished situation
D. when the organism repents
E. in man because man has a moral nature

76. Skinner feels that in studying verbal behavior, speech sounds

A. must be analyzed with concepts different from those usually applied to behavior since speech is symbolic
B. cannot be handled with the same concepts used in other behavior because speech sounds are subjective responses of the person
C. are too complex to be analyzed as is other behavior
D. are emitted and reinforced as any other behavior and are thus subject to analysis by the same concepts used for all operant behavior
E. can be studied only through formal structural linguistics

77. For Hull, the contiguity between stimulus and response occurs

A. inside the organism
B. outside the organism
C. both inside and outside the organism bringing the two areas together
D. in none of the above situations
E. in mental images

78. For Hull, an S-R connection is learned

A. only because it occurs in an association with reinforcement
B. because it enables the organism to function
C. when the situation in which the S-R connection was experienced is immediately changed
D. as a result of the expectation of the organism
E. without drive reduction

79. In his later formulations, Hull contends that the only systematic influence on sHr (habit strength) is

A. the amount of delay between response and reinforcement
B. the drive level
C. conditioned inhibition
D. the probability of the response occurring
E. the number of reinforced trials

80. Skinner proposes that the most useful psychological theory is

A. a hypothetico-deductive theory
B. an inductive theory describing the functional relationships found in the data
C. one that finds explanations on a level other than psychological
D. one using a physiological explanation
E. based on a mathematical model

81. According to Hull, fractional-anticipatory goal responses

A. give rise to stimuli which act as surrogates for directing ideas
B. give rise to stimuli which generate the gradient of reinforcement
C. give rise to stimuli important in secondary reinforcement
D. may do all of the above
E. may do both A and C

82. In Hull's theory of learning, reactive inhibition (Ir) is generated

A. only when a motor response occurs
B. only when an emotional response occurs
C. only during extinction
D. whenever a response is made
E. only during acquisition

83. According to Skinner, a drive is

A. a stimulus
B. a physiological state
C. a psychic state
D. a need state
E. none of the above

84. The typical psychopath exhibits

A. sexual deviations directed toward specific erotic pleasure
B. high threshold for alcohol
C. apparent immunity to remorse
D. delinquency limited to a particular sphere of behavior
E. childish speech

85. A high correlation coefficient or coefficient of determination between an independent variable and a dependent variable indicates that

A. a cause and effect relationship may exist
B. a cause and effect relationship exists
C. a change in the dependent variable is caused by a change in the independent variable
D. a change in the independent variable is caused by a change in the dependent variable
E. a cause and effect relationship cannot exist

86. For Guthrie the motivational state of the organism

A. is basic because his reinforcement theory depends on it
B. is more important than what the organism does
C. is important because it determines the vigor and presence of the movements that will become associated in learning
D. is important because of his formal assumption that drive reduction occurs during learning
E. is less important than the emotional state

87. According to Skinner, a chained response

A. is very rarely found in ordinary behavior
B. is a part of all operant behavior
C. can be observed only under special laboratory situations
D. is a hypothetical construct
E. occurs only in pigeons

88. Hue refers to

A. purity
B. intensity
C. wavelength
D. saturation
E. brightness

89. Skinner describes "superstitious behavior"

A. as a hangover from "mentalistic" psychology
B. as occurring when there is an accidental connection between a response and reinforcer
C. as never having been observed in an experimental situation
D. as not occurring in human beings
E. by either A or C

90. In general, in experiments in which one group of rats was run in a maze for several days and rewarded with food at the end of each run, and another group was run for the same number of days without food reward at the end of the runs,

1. it was found that when food was given the second group, error scores and time scores became abruptly alike for both groups
2. it was found that when food was given the second group, the error and time scores of that group indicated poorer performance than that of the first group

3. it was concluded that the second group had apparently profited as much from its unfed trials as the first group had profited from its fed trials

A. 1 and 2 took place
B. 2 and 3 took place
C. 1 and 3 took place
D. 1, 2, and 3 took place
E. none of the above took place

91. As the word "sample" is used in statistical terminology, it refers to a subset of a

A. mean
B. study group
C. normal curve
D. population
E. random sample

92. According to Abraham Maslow

A. man's inborn nature is essentially evil
B. the needs of man are evil and must be tamed by society
C. a passion is a natural instinct of man
D. the inborn nature of man is essentially good
E. behavior is largely determined instinctually

93. In Kretschmer's classification of people according to physique types, the fragile, linear, lean, thin-stomached individual is classified as

A. athletic
B. somatotonic
C. pyknic
D. dyplastic
E. aesthenic

94. The term "biosphere," which refers to the idea of viewing the person and his environment as a holistic entity, separable only by abstraction, was coined by

A. Kurt Goldstein
B. Gordon Allport
C. A. Angyal
D. Carl Rogers
E. Erich Fromm

95. In linguistic terminology, the suffix "ing" is

A. a morpheme
B. a phoneme
C. a phone
D. an allophone
E. an infix

96. The technique of psychodrama as a part of psychotherapy was developed by

A. Freud
B. Sullivan
C. Fromm
D. Jung
E. Moreno

97. According to Kurt Goldstein, an individual is primarily motivated by

A. an infinite number of secondary drives that become autonomous
B. a set of 12 primary drives
C. both primary drives and secondary drives which are directly related to them
D. a single motive which is called self-actualization or self-realization
E. a set of 9 primary needs

98. A person making a primarily <u>idiographic</u> study of behavior would

A. focus his study on the individual, using methods appropriate for studying individual cases
B. use a large number of variables and many subjects
C. focus on general principles over a large range of subjects
D. emphasize general trends that can be statistically predicted for a large group of subjects
E. attempt to verify one hypothesis at a time

99. In their study of expressive movement Allport and Vernon concluded that

A. they were unable to find habits of gesture which were stable characteristics of their subjects
B. habits of gesture were stable characteristics of their subjects

C. no consistency in scores for tasks done with particular left and particular right muscle groups could be found
D. while there was some consistency among particular scores, correlations among the major variables suggest no generality underlying scores
E. habits of gesture were stable characteristics for only left handed subjects

100. Allport states that a person whose present motives are linked to the past and to biological states

A. is likely to be more mature than a person whose motives are more autonomous
B. is likely to be less mature than a person whose motives are more autonomous
C. is more likely to be an adult than a child
D. is functionally autonomous
E. is extremely mature

101. According to Allport's principle of functional autonomy,

A. a piece of behavior may be continued as a result of a motive other than the one that gave rise to the behavior
B. a piece of behavior may become a goal in itself even if the behavior began as a response to a particular motive
C. a piece of behavior may become a goal in itself only if it did not begin as a response to a particular motive
D. a piece of behavior continues because of a connection to the motive that originally gave rise to it
E. some behavior occurs in the absence of any motivation whatsoever

102. Client-centered therapy is most typically associated with

A. Carl Rogers
B. C. G. Jung
C. Alfred Adler
D. Otto Fenichel
E. Karen Horney

103. According to Sullivan, superstitious behavior is an example of

A. protaxic experience
B. parataxic experience
C. syntaxic experience
D. intaxic experience
E. propotaxic experience

104. Below are questions, all but one of which are designed to be helpful in determining the usefullness and validity of a published research report. Which is the misfit?

A. Are all pertinent and relevant data adequately and understandably presented?
B. Does the author adequately describe the nature of additional research suggested by the results?
C. Are results of statistical tests expressed in terms of probability of the influence of chance on results?
D. Are graphs and charts used adequately and are they sufficiently complete?
E. None of the above.

105. The term "personology" was introduced into personality theory by

A. Sullivan B. Fromm
C. Murray D. Adler
E. Horney

106. That value of a variable which occurs most often is the

A. standard deviation
B. mean
C. mode
D. median
E. average deviation

107. Which of the following are the types of factors, other than factors under direct investigation, which can influence the nature or degree of the results of a clinical research study?

1. basic differences between populations being compared
2. poor sampling techniques
3. poor study control
4. inappropriate examination criteria

A. 1 only
B. 1 and 3
C. 2, 3, and 4
D. 1, 3, and 4
E. all of the above

108. In contrast to Freud, Horney feels that the Oedipus complex

A. is an anxiety resulting from deep disturbances in the child's relationship with his parents, rather than a sexual-aggressive conflict
B. is purely a sexual conflict with no aggressive impulses expressed
C. is never the result of parental rejection of the child
D. is the result of parental overprotection rather than excess punishment
E. none of the above

109. The pattern of sampling variability is known if the sampling is

A. the result of "expert" judgment
B. biased
C. a mixture of expert selection and random sampling
D. from two related populations
E. random

110. Which one of the following is not true about a normal distribution?

A. It is represented by a bell-shaped curve.
B. It has one mode.
C. The mode and the mean are equal.
D. The mean and the median are equal.
E. It has two modes.

111. A question to which a person is asked to respond "yes," "no," or "don't know" is an example of

A. an open-ended question
B. a fixed alternative question
C. a free-response question
D. a recall question
E. a non-structured question

112. Henry Murray is famous for having developed

A. the Rorschach Test
B. the MMPI
C. the Role Concept Repertory Test
D. the process of factor analysis
E. the Thematic Apperception Test

113. In a distribution of 35 values, the 36th value changes the mean of the first 35 values

A. by 1/6 of the difference which exists between the 36th value and the old mean
B. by 1/36 of the difference which exists between the 36th value and the old mean
C. by 1/2 of the difference which exists between the 36th value and the old mean
D. not at all
E. by 1/4 of the difference which exists between the 36th value and the old mean

114. Using a four-sided die, (each side having the digit 1, 2, 3, or 4 on it) the probability of getting first a 2 and then a 4 on two consecutive tosses of the die is

A. one out of 8
B. one out of 2
C. one out of 4
D. one out of 12
E. one out of 16

115. If an experimenter statistically tested the difference between two means, he would be likely to have the most confidence in the difference between them if he found them to be different

A. at a .05 significance level
B. at a .1 significance level
C. at a .01 significance level
D. at a .001 significance level
E. at a .50 significance level

116. According to Jung, the persona of a person

A. is the feminine archetype of the man
B. consists of the animal instincts inherited through evolution
C. is the role expected of him by society
D. is responsible for the appearance of socially unacceptable feelings
E. is racially inherited

117. Evidence from Lipset and Bendix's studies of changes in social mobility in modern industrial societies indicates that

A. there is much less chance of upward social mobility at the present time than there was in the early nineteenth century
B. there is much more social mobility in the U.S.A. than in other western countries
C. there has been little change in the amount of upward social mobility from the early nineteenth century to the present
D. there is much less social mobility in the U.S.A. than in other western countries
E. there is an equal amount of upward social mobility in the U.S.A. as compared with other western countries

118. From the theory of relative deprivation, one may predict that

A. in a high mobility system, people are less likely to be critical and feel frustrated about their chances for movement or promotion
B. if a person fails to achieve an attractive goal, his morale will be higher with the belief that the chances of his obtaining the goal had been quite high
C. if a person fails to achieve an attractive goal, his morale will be lower with the belief that the chances of his obtaining the goal had been quite high
D. in a low mobility system, people are more likely to be critical of their present position
E. level of aspiration depends on upward mobility in the society

119. A questionnaire made up of such items as "I would willingly admit members of X-group to my club, to my country, or to kinship by marriage," would probably be yielding data to form

A. a Likert scale
B. a Thurstone attitude scale
C. a scale-discrimination technique
D. a Gutman scale
E. a Bogardus social distance sale

120. The study, "The Authoritarian Personality," by Frenkel-Brunswik, Adorno, Levinson, and Sanford

A. investigated the personality correlates of prejudice
B. investigated moral attitudes of American soldiers during World War II
C. investigated attitudes toward labor-management relations
D. investigated the effects of child-rearing practices on toleration of frustration
E. investigated the personalities of company executives

121. "A kind of sampling in which definite parts of the total sample are allocated to definite parts, or strata, of the population" is a definition of

A. random sampling
B. selective sampling
C. discrete sampling
D. stratified sampling
E. none of the above

122. An investigator asking people how they classify themselves and others in the status system of a community is using

A. the objective method of determining social class

B. the subjective method of determining social class
C. the reputational method of determining social class
D. a combination of the subjective and objective method of determining social class
E. the structural method of determining social class

123. Using the social area method, Tyron has attempted to

A. specify the neighborhoods of different social strata
B. investigate morale of the American soldier
C. investigate the effects of child-rearing practices on reactions to fear
D. investigate the interpersonal situations a child faces in a normal day
E. determine SES in New Haven

124. Pavlov's law of conditioning is clearly a statement of a (an)

A. reinforcement theory
B. field theory
C. color theory
D. organismic theory
E. contiguity theory

125. In total color blindness, all wavelengths and all mixtures

1. differ in brightness
2. differ in hue

A. 1 is correct; 2 is incorrect
B. 1 is incorrect; 2 is correct
C. both 1 and 2 are correct
D. neither 1 nor 2 is correct
E. 1 is always correct; 2 is correct only for red-green color blindness

Answer questions 126-127-128 with reference to the passage quoted below.

The patient spoke lucidly about the world that she lived in. She reported that she was being watched constantly by both neighbors and government officials, who know that she has rare powers of both prophesying the future and exerting complete control over the weather. She also reported that her children are in league with the others, and constantly are trying to poison her food. After she spoke, her case was diagnosed by the attending psychiatrist.

126. The most probable diagnosis of this woman's case is

A. simple schizophrenia
B. paranoid schizophrenia
C. hebephrenic schizophrenia
D. manic-depressive psychosis
E. catatonic schizophrenia

127. The probable symtoms that the doctor based his diagnosis on were

A. silliness
B. delusions of grandeur
C. bizarre mood shifts
D. feelings of persecution
E. both B and D

128. If the patient described above had lucidly reported that she was afraid of water because she felt she would drown, she would be classified as

A. hebephrenic
B. manic-depressive
C. anxiety neurotic
D. paranoid
E. paranoid schizophrenic

129. The best synonym for the term <u>reliability</u> is

A. validity
B. consistency
C. temporality
D. truth
E. contemporaneity

130. In statistical terminology, a straight-line correlation is one

A. in which a change in one factor is consistently accompanied by a proportionate change in a second factor
B. in which, to have statistical significance, the coefficient of correlation must be in a range of 0.05 or less

C. in which there is a correlation ratio of 1.00 and a positive straight-line proportion between two factors
D. in which there is a correlation ratio of -1.00 and a negative straight-line proportion between two factors
E. none of the above

131. The type of validity which predicts success or failure in specific situations is

A. content validity
B. construct validity
C. face validity
D. criterion validity
E. synthetic validity

132. The one characteristic that particularly differentiates neurotic behavior from sociopathy is that

A. in neurosis, the main victim is the patient
B. in neurosis, there are no feelings of unreality
C. sociopaths misinterpret external reality
D. neurotics have no compulsive rituals
E. sociopaths suffer from great personality disorganization

Answer questions 133-136 with reference to the passage quoted below.

Psychology must study scientifically the behavior of organisms. Therefore the field of animal behavior is legitimately included in the field of psychology. We can no sooner infer consciousness from the behavior of animals than we can from the behavior of humans. The same methods used to study animal behavior can be used to study human behavior. The psychologist studying human behavior, just as the psychologist studying animal behavior, can have no access to the consciousness of the subject, and therefore cannot scientifically infer consciousness from his experimental observations or data.

133. This point of view holds that

A. conscious experience does not exist
B. introspective reports should be taken as descriptions of conscious experience
C. introspective reports are objective
D. conscious experience cannot be studied scientifically
E. both A and D are true

134. A psychologist expressing the view given in the paragraph holds that

A. animal behavior is a valid subject for study in its own right
B. animal behavior should be studied to gain information about animal consciousness
C. animal behavior should be studied only to develop methods for studying human behavior
D. animal behavior should be studied because of the light it sheds on human behavior
E. animal behavior should be studied in preference to human behavior

135. The point of view expressed above could best be called

A. structuralism
B. objective functionalism
C. introspection
D. holism
E. none of the above

136. A psychologist holding the theoretical position expressed above would be most likely to describe behavior in terms of

A. underlying images
B. stimuli and observable responses
C. symbolic acts
D. decision processes
E. none of the above

137. A once influential lawyer and judge was admitted to the hospital after attempting to convince people on the street that he had found <u>the</u> cure for cancer. The patient's cancer "cure" considered of "changing the electrical balance of the cells of the body." He attempted to write to the governor of the state, explaining this discovery, and also

wrote to heads of large corporations (like General Motors) as well. When he received no replies, he felt the Communists were interfering and tampering with his mail. His diagnosis would most likely be

A. simple schizophrenia
B. paranoid schizophrenia--suspicious type
C. paranoid schizophrenia--grandiose type
D. paranoid schizophrenia--mixed type
E. paranoid schizophrenia--delusional type

Answer questions 138-142 with reference to the passage quoted below.

Many psychologists interested in drives are concerned with the effect of manipulations of primary drives on performance of subjects. These psychologists are concerned with creating empirical laws to relate independent motivational variables to dependent behavior. Among the problems that have been studied in detail are the effects of deprivation on consummatory behavior and on instrumental behavior.

138. Consummatory behavior includes

A. pressing a bar
B. behavior on an activity wheel
C. eating
D. salivation
E. all of the above

139. The empirical relation between water deprivation and drinking behavior has been shown to be

A. an increasing, negatively accelerated function of deprivation time for periods up to 48 hours
B. an increasing, positively accelerated function of deprivation time for periods up to 48 hours
C. an increasing, directly accelerated function of deprivation time for periods up to 48 hours
D. an increasing, negatively accelerated function of deprivation time for periods up to 72 hours
E. an increasing, directly accelerated function of deprivation time for periods of up to 72 hours

140. If animals which had been maintained on a 24 hour feeding schedule <u>prior</u> to a deprivation regime were to be divided into 2 groups, one deprived for 18 and the other for 24 hours and the latter group were to eat more, we might conclude that

A. associative strengths between the two groups were not held constant
B. the group deprived longer had higher drive
C. there was no difference in associative strength between the two groups
D. both A and B are reasonable conclusions
E. both B and C are reasonable conclusions

141. The most comprehensive design to test the effect of differing motivational levels on extinction would be

A. all groups are under identical conditions during acquisition and different conditions during extinction
B. all groups are under different conditions during acquisition and the same condition during extinction
C. only half the subjects are given extinction training, following acquisition
D. extinction is measured from the operant, rather than from the acquisition level for half the subjects
E. subjects are given extensive training during acquisition under <u>all</u> the levels of deprivation to be used in the extinction condition

142. The relationship between choice of the correct side in a T-maze experiment and food deprivation has been shown to

A. be monotonically related to time of deprivation
B. indicate no systematic relation to deprivation time
C. depend on the class of animals used as subjects
D. depend on whether the animals are forced to the non-rewarded side as often as the rewarded side and on whether or not they are forced to rectify their errors
E. be a non-monotonic, curvilinear function of deprivation time

Answer questions 143-146 with reference to the diagram shown below.

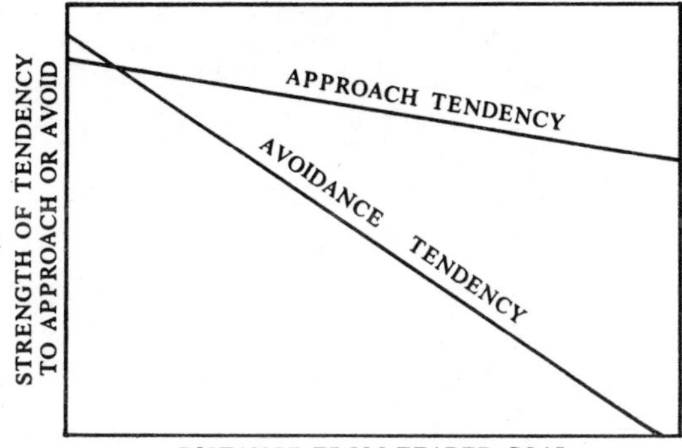

143. The model shown above does not assume that

A. the gradient of avoidance is steeper than the gradient of approach
B. both approach and avoidance tendencies become stronger the nearer the individual is to the goal
C. increase in drive level raises approach tendencies, but not avoidance tendencies
D. increase in drive level will raise the gradients of both approach and avoidance
E. if there are two competing responses present, the stronger one will occur

144. This model considers that competition between two approach responses

A. is an insoluble dilemma
B. will end with the occurrence of an avoidance response
C. will end as soon as the individual starts to move to one or the other goal
D. will be soluble only when the approach responses are not equally balanced initially
E. is true in the cases of B and D

145. The theoretical position of the above model rests on

A. reinforcement only
B. contiguity only
C. reinforcement and contiguity
D. expectancy
E. none of the above

146. At the point of intersection of the two gradients, in the diagram, we would not expect conflict to develop

A. if the approach response is stronger than the avoidance response
B. if the avoidance response is stronger than the approach response
C. if approach and avoidance tendencies are equally matched
D. in both B and C
E. in both A and B

Answer questions 147-148-149 with reference to the passage quoted below.

Adams and Rosenbaum showed that subjects overcompensated by the hour show a greater productivity than those paid by the hour who felt fairly compensated; overcompensated workers paid by the piece showed lower productivity than those who were told that they were paid fairly.

147. The experimenters take this experiment to verify their theory of

A. social influence
B. social comparison
C. equity

D. social conformity
E. none of the above

148. The overcompensated piece-workers are showing lower productivity in order to

A. reduce the discrepancy between expectation and outcome
B. retaliate toward management
C. show they are inferior to the other workers
D. do all of the above
E. do none of the above

149. The theory presented would expect a person either to raise or lower his inputs when the inputs are

A. in a complementary relationship to those of other workers
B. too high relative to those of other workers
C. too low relative to those of other workers
D. in an obverse relationship to those of other workers
E. in none of the above situations

Answer questions 150-153 with reference to the passage quoted below.

American psychology has, in general, been environmentally oriented. However, personality theory must be constitutionally oriented in order to provide a scientific basis for the description of human behavior. The basis of such a psychology, then, involves units by which the physical structure of the body and behavior can be quantitatively measured and related to each other. It is imperative to look to the biological substratum of the individual for the factors which will be vital in influencing behavior.

150. In the constitutional psychology of Sheldon, the three primary components of physique are

A. endomorphy, ectomorphy and mesomorphy
B. endomorphy, mesomorphy and pyknic
C. ectomorphy, mesomorphy and leptosome
D. endomorphy, ectomorphy and leptosome
E. endomorphy, ectomorphy and pyknic

151. According to Sheldon, there is a correlation between body type and temperament so that

A. endomorphs are viscerotonic
B. ectomophs are viscerotonic
C. ectomorphs are cerebrotonic
D. mesomorphs are viscerotonic
E. both A and C are true

152. Somatotonia is characterized by

A. gluttony for food, people, and affection
B. need for strong muscular and physical activity
C. a need for restraint and concealment
D. chronic anxiety
E. high verbal ability

153. The constitutional psychologist accepts the notion that

A. there are no unconscious processes
B. unconscious factors are really biological forces impelling the body
C. the effect of early events on adult behavior is the result of the operation of similar biological forces over time
D. constitutional psychologists have yet to comment on either the unconscious or the effects of early experience
E. both B and C are true

Answer questions 154-155-156 with reference to the diagram shown on the following page.

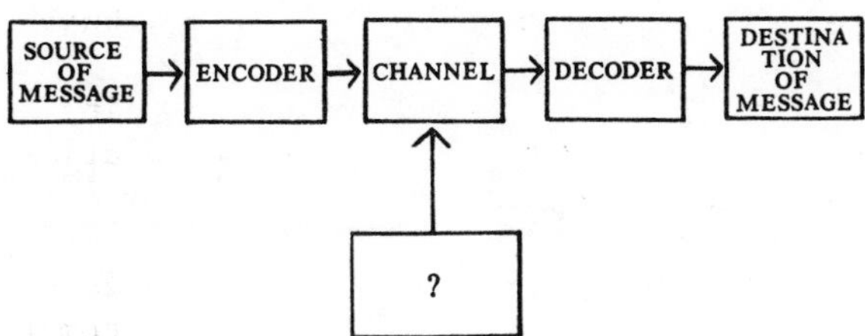

154. The illustration shown above represents

A. Shannon's communication theory
B. Skinner's communication theory
C. Von Newmann's game theory in a communication situation
D. Estes communication theory
E. Wiener's communication theory

155. The box with the question mark represents

A. the particular media employed
B. the conditions at the time of message transmission
C. general noise (or interference)
D. all of the above
E. both A and C

156. If we were to make the above model analagous to a learning situation, we could best consider the two end points (source and destination respectively) as

A. observable responses and the observing psychologist
B. the observing psychologist and observable responses
C. stimulus conditions and observable responses
D. observable responses and stimulus conditions
E. stimulus conditions and the observing psychologist

Answer questions 157-158 with reference to the diagram shown below.

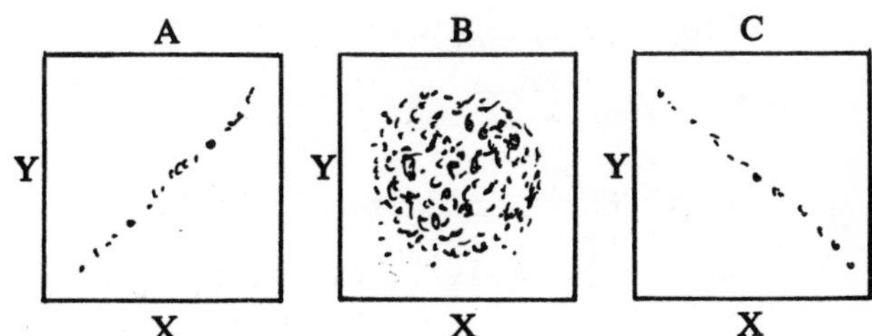

157. The x and the y axis are referred to respectively as

A. ordinate and abcissa
B. abcissa and ordinate
C. abcissa and linear axis
D. ordinate and linear axis
E. none of the above

158. The size of a correlation will be decreased if

A. the x variable is sampled from a homogeneous population
B. the y variable is sampled from a homogeneous population
C. the x variable is sampled from a heterogeneous population
D. the y variable is sampled from a heterogeneous population
E. both A and B are true

Answer questions 159-163 with reference to the passage quoted below.

In general, contemporary theorists on motivation distinguish between those independent variables that motivate (or activate) behavior, and those that guide (or direct) behavior. For example, variables such as drives, motivations, and libidos are considered activators; associative tendencies and habit strength are considered as directive agents. However, there are certain manipulative variables that exert both an energizing and a directive function on behavior. To meet with the problems offered by such variables, several theoretical reinterpretations have been offered.

159. One satisfactory solution to the dynamic-directive problem has been

   A. to consider reinforcement and ignore activation completely
   B. to consider drive as a motivator, and provide separate sensory stimuli which are directive
   C. to assume that drive itself guides behavior
   D. all of the above
   E. none of the above

160. According to Hull, the relationship between drive (D) and habit strength (sHr) which yields excitatory potential is

   A. multiplicative
   B. additive
   C. logarithmic
   D. exponential
   E. none of the above

161. Hull's conception of drive holds that

   A. drive facilitates all ongoing activity
   B. drive interacts with associative tendencies to produce excitatory potential
   C. different drives result from different stimulation
   D. both A and B are true
   E. both B and C are true

162. A secondary drive differs from a primary drive in that

   A. it is always of weaker intensity
   B. it is usually a learned drive
   C. it is satisfied by different stimuli than a primary drive, in general
   D. all of the above are true
   E. B and C are true

163. The variable which was stressed by Spence and not considered in detail by Hull is

   A. habit strength
   B. oscillation
   C. fractional anticipatory goal responses
   D. incentive
   E. conditioned inhibition

Answer questions 164-165-166 with reference to the passage quoted below.

A concept is defined as an abstraction which provides some unifying feature to a seemingly diverse set of objects. Concepts develop through processes of abstraction together with generalization. Once formed, these concepts shape the way in which we, to a large extent, see the world. In forming concepts, different things are grouped according to such common attributes as size, shape, color, frequency of occurrence and usage. Experiments frequently demand that subjects give the same "name" to a class of objects grouped according to a certain concept.

164. From the information given in the above paragraph, we would expect poorer concept formation to be shown by children, schizophrenics, and brain-damaged adults because of

   A. lower levels of abstracting abilities
   B. lower levels of intelligence
   C. higher levels of chronic anxiety
   D. both A and B
   E. none of the above

165. All of the following psychologists have done work in concept formation <u>except</u>

   A. Hull
   B. Heidbreder
   C. Bruner
   D. Skinner
   E. Hovland

166. In order to develop a concept,

   A. many instances of the class should be presented and associated with the common feature
   B. only one member of the class should be presented as illustrating the common feature
   C. examples of classes which the common feature does <u>not</u> pertain to, should be presented
   D. all of the above are equally good strategies for teaching concept formation
   E. B and C are the best strategies for teaching concept formation

167. The method of correlation for ranked data is

   A. Pearson product moment correlation
   B. Kendall's tau
   C. Spearman's rho
   D. Kendall's zeta
   E. multiple correlation

Answer questions 168-169 with reference to the passage quoted below.

If three candles are burning in a dark room, and we add a fourth, the brightening effect of this candle will be most apparent. Suppose we have 75 candles burning in a dark room. Now, the effect of another one is just barely noticeable. If there are 500 candles burning and another one is added, no change, at all, will be noticed.

168. The smallest stimulus that a subject can receive and then report a change in the previously existing level of stimulation is called

   A. light constancy
   B. size constancy
   C. just-noticeable difference
   D. contextual illusion
   E. none of the above

169. Whether one will discriminate a difference between stimulus a and stimulus b depends on

   A. the absolute magnitude of a and b
   B. the relative magnitude of a and b
   C. an exponetial relationship between a and b
   D. what proportion the change from a to b is of a
   E. none of the above

Answer questions 170-171-172 with reference to the passage quoted below.

In a psychological experiment, the investigator must take into account factors such as the nature of the organisms to be studied, the responses already existing in the repertory of this organism, as well as the existing condition of this organism. He must also carefully plan the stimuli to be presented in the experiment, take account of other stimuli possibly operating in the situation, and carefully decide which of the responses on the part of the organism are to be measured.

170. The stimulus (or organic) conditions which are manipulated by the experimenter are called

   A. independent variables
   B. dependent variables
   C. intervening variables
   D. hypothetical constructs
   E. antecendent conditions

171. All of the following are examples of organic independent variables <u>except</u>

   A. age
   B. cerebral development
   C. sex
   D. force exerted on a lever by the hand (or paw) of the organism
   E. hunger of the organism

172. Counterbalancing is used in experimental design

A. to insure equal number of subjects in control and experimental conditions
B. to maintain a constant dependent variable for both experimental and control subjects
C. to insure against progressive effects during the course of the experiment
D. in both A and C
E. in both B and C

Answer questions 173-174 with reference to the passage quoted below.

The adult traits will be ultimately dependent on a combination of the factors of heredity and environment. Psychologists involved in the so-called "nature-nurture" controversy have been fortunate in that they are able to use identical twins and so hold the heredity constant; however, they have been less fortunate in their effort to hold the environment constant for any two human beings.

173. Environment cannot be held constant for any two people because

A. proper methods for doing so have not yet been developed
B. psychologists cannot account for all factors in any environment
C. individuals select out different aspects of the same environment
D. of both B and C
E. of none of the above

174. Hebb's view of the nature-nurture controversy is that

A. heredity is more important than environment
B. environment is more important than heredity
C. environment is <u>all</u>-important
D. heredity and environment interact, so that it is impossible to determine the precise contribution of each
E. none of the above is true

Answer questions 175-178 with reference to the passage quoted below.

The clinical notion of projection is manifested whenever we attribute our feelings to other people or to other objects. The projective test asks the individual to place himself in the testing framework; that is, to identify with the characters or situation in the test, and, by naming their feelings about what is going on in the situation, he will be giving his <u>own</u> feelings for the psychologist to measure. The projective tests devised to date include inkblot tests, interpretation of various pictures or cartoons, doll play and sentence completion. Despite seeming difference, such tests have many underlying features in common.

175. The Thematic Apperception Test is based on the principle that

A. different meanings will emerge from different photographs presented as stimuli
B. different meanings will emerge between subjects on the same photograph, since they bring different experience to bear on their perception
C. projection can be better demonstrated with concrete stimuli such as photographs of people
D. projection can be better demonstrated with abstract stimuli, such as the combination of line drawing and inkblot
E. none of the above are true

176. The best example of an item on a sentence-completion projective test is

A. All men are created free and ________.
B. It is better to have loved and lost than never ________.
C. ________ wouldn't melt in his mouth.
D. The aim of life is ___________.
E. Absence makes the heart _______.

177. All of the following entities are scored on the Rorschach except

A. number of items seen
B. reported conversations between items or people
C. whole-part relationships between items
D. color and form
E. movement

178. The strongest criticism of projective tests is based on

A. ambiguity of interpretation of response
B. narrow range of potential responses which may be elicited
C. failure to provide hypotheses about human motivation
D. lack of quantification of responses
E. both A and D

179. Tryon's study of breeding selectivity for maze learning in rats showed that

A. after seven generations of breeding bright with bright and dull with dull rats, there was a bi-modal curve of maze learning ability
B. after seven generations of such selective breeding, there were very few rats with intermediate maze-learning ability
C. when selectively-bred bright rats were bred with selectively bred dull rats, the resulting generation had intermediate maze learning ability
D. all of the above are true
E. none of the above is true

180. A psychologist would desire that a test show low test-retest reliability if

A. he were developing a test to differentiate personality groups
B. he were conducting an attitude survey
C. he were conducting an attitude change experiment
D. both A and C are true
E. both B and C are true

Answer questions 181-185 with reference to the diagram shown below.

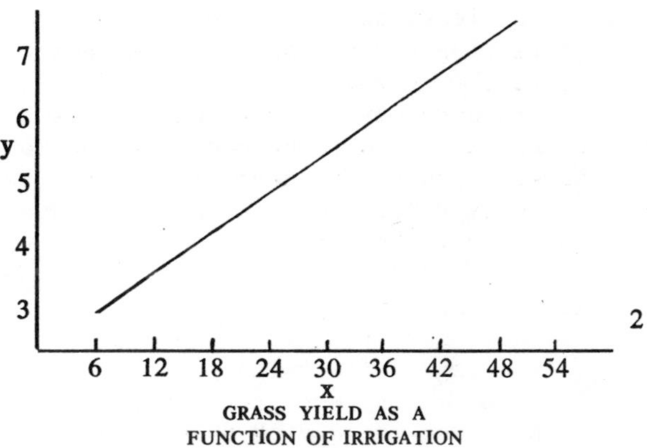

GRASS YIELD AS A FUNCTION OF IRRIGATION

181. The regression relationship shown above

A. assumes that a theoretical straight line expresses the linear relationship between the theoretical mean value of x and of y

B. we can predict the value of y from the known value of x
C. is linear and monotonic
D. applies to all of the above
E. applies to none of the above

182. Correlation differs from regression because

A. only regression can be used for prediction
B. regression is used to express (only) the relationship between two variables
C. correlation is used to discover how variables are linearly related
D. both A and B
E. both A and C

183. The least squares technique of fitting a regression line allows

A. x values to be fixed in advance
B. x values to be chosen from the population under study
C. y values to be chosen in advance
D. y values to be chosen from the population sampled
E. all three, A, B and D

184. The regression fallacy is

A. associated with the interpretations of data taken at different periods of time
B. associated with interpretations of data taken simultaneously
C. not theoretically connected with the regression line shown above
D. applicable to all of the above
E. applicable to none of the above

185. The regression fallacy indicates

A. that mean groups will shift to the extremes
B. that extreme groups will shift to the mean
C. extreme groups are similar to each other and different from mean groups
D. both A and C are true
E. both B and C are true

Answer questions 186-190 with reference to the passage quoted below.

One of the fundamental problems of statistics is testing hypotheses about populations. For example, physical anthropologists have discovered that in tribe A, the mean head length is 194 centimeters; in tribe B, it is 200 centimeters. The standard deviations of head length is the same for both groups (about 8 centimeters). The anthropologists discover another small tribe (only 12 in number) that they think is really part of tribe A. The mean head length of this group of 12 is 198 centimeters. The anthropologists ask a statistician to test the hypothesis that the 12 men belong to tribe A rather than to tribe B.

186. If the 12 men really do belong to tribe A

A. their population's true mean is 194 centimeters head length
B. their population's true mean is 200 centimeters head length
C. their population's true mean is 198 centimeters head length
D. no statement can be made about the true population mean for head length
E. none of the above statements is true

187. If the hypothesis that the 12 men belong to tribe A were rejected <u>incorrectly</u>

A. the statistician would have made a Type I error
B. the statistician would have made a Type II error
C. the statistician would be guilty of the regression fallacy
D. both A and C are true
E. both B and C are true

188. The problem presented above is unusual in that

A. the statistician usually does not have 2 simple alternatives as to what the true mean may be
B. the usual case holds that all other possible values might be the true mean

C. the usual case does not specify whether the true mean is larger or smaller than the mean being tested
D. all of the above are true
E. none of the above is true

189. In order to solve the problem presented above, we must begin by considering the standard deviation of the mean of the samples. This is computed by

A. dividing the standard deviation by the square root of N
B. dividing the standard deviation by N
C. dividing the variance by the square root of N
D. dividing the variance by N
E. both A and D

190. The graphs of the curves of the two means would be assumed to be

A. normally distributed
B. both skewed positively
C. both skewed negatively
D. both in a F distribution
E. both in a chi-square distribution

Answer questions 191-192 with reference to the table shown below.

INTERVAL	F
90-99	1
80-89	5
70-79	8
60-69	7
50-59	8
40-49	5
30-39	3
20-29	1
	38

191. The distribution shown most closely approximates the

A. normal distribution
B. hypergeometric distribution
C. binomial distribution
D. F distribution
E. chi-square distribution

192. A plot of cumulative frequency differs from a non-cumulative frequency plot in that

A. cumulative curves use the upper boundary of the interval in plotting
B. cumulative curves use the midpoint of the interval in the plot
C. non-cumulative curves use the midpoint of the interval in plotting
D. non-cumulative curves use the lower boundary of the interval in plotting
E. both A and C are true

Answer questions 193-196 with reference to the passage quoted below.

As the personality develops, the ego becomes more differentiated in structure and it secures greater control over the more instinctual sources of energy. The various systems of the personality becomes integrated. Through learning, the mechanisms of identification, displacement, defenses, and sublimation, the person is able to cope with frustrations and anxieties.

193. The process by which energy is channeled from one object to another higher cultural object is called

A. displacement
B. fusion of instinct
C. sublimation
D. projection
E. condensation

194. A person experiences an extreme degree of anxiety in the presence of a specific other person. He, nontheless, appears to act very friendly in the presence of this person. This defense is known as

A. sublimation
B. reaction
C. repression
D. fixation
E. rationalization

195. Ego defenses originally exist because

   A. the infantile ego cannot cope with anxiety by rational means
   B. the infantile ego cannot cope with the demands made on it
   C. they channel ego energy into a rational mold
   D. of both A and B
   E. of both B and C

196. A person expressing the view in the preceding paragraph would agree that actions are based on all the following factors <u>except</u>

   A. direct expression of instincts
   B. a drive unconnected with the life or death instinct
   C. combinations of instincts
   D. compromises of instincts
   E. ego defenses

Answer questions 197-200 with reference to the passage quoted below.

We cannot simply speak of a test in terms of how reliable or how valid it is. In terms of reliability, it is necessary to consider the nature of the measures of reliability used. In terms of validity, we must ask: valid for what?--and so we must look at the validity of the test in terms of what its use will eventually be based on.

197. Reliabilities can be ascertained by

   A. giving the same subject similar tests at different times
   B. giving the same subject equivalent forms of the same test at different times
   C. using the same test on the same subject at different times
   D. both A and B
   E. both B and C

198. All the following statements are true of reliability coefficients <u>except</u>

   A. the coefficient depends on the range of scores in the group under study
   B. the coefficient depends on the length of the test under consideration
   C. the coefficient is an equally good measure at all levels of ability
   D. the coefficient describes what proportion of the test variance is not error variance
   E. the <u>validity</u> coefficient cannot be higher than the square root of the reliability coefficient

199. Increasing test length

   A. has a greater effect on reliability than on validity
   B. has a greater effect on validity than on reliability
   C. has an equal effect on both reliability and on validity
   D. effects <u>only</u> reliability
   E. effects <u>only</u> validity

200. A psychological theoretician in the process of developing a theory would be most interested in test measures in terms of their

   A. face validity
   B. predictive validity
   C. concurrent validity
   D. construct validity
   E. none of the above

SAMPLE TEST 1

ANSWER KEY

1.	D	41.	D	81.	D	121.	D	161.	D
2.	A	42.	E	82.	D	122.	C	162.	E
3.	B	43.	D	83.	E	123.	A	163.	D
4.	C	44.	A	84.	C	124.	E	164.	A
5.	E	45.	B	85.	A	125.	A	165.	D
6.	E	46.	C	86.	C	126.	B	166.	A
7.	C	47.	A	87.	B	127.	E	167.	C
8.	B	48.	B	88.	C	128.	E	168.	C
9.	C	49.	A	89.	B	129.	B	169.	B
10.	B	50.	B	90.	C	130.	A	170.	A
11.	C	51.	C	91.	D	131.	D	171.	D
12.	B	52.	D	92.	D	132.	A	172.	C
13.	E	53.	B	93.	E	133.	D	173.	D
14.	B	54.	A	94.	C	134.	A	174.	D
15.	C	55.	E	95.	A	135.	B	175.	B
16.	C	56.	C	96.	E	136.	B	176.	D
17.	B	57.	B	97.	D	137.	D	177.	B
18.	E	58.	E	98.	A	138.	C	178.	E
19.	C	59.	B	99.	B	139.	A	179.	D
20.	B	60.	C	100.	B	140.	D	180.	C
21.	E	61.	B	101.	B	141.	E	181.	D
22.	A	62.	D	102.	A	142.	D	182.	E
23.	A	63.	A	103.	B	143.	C	183.	E
24.	E	64.	D	104.	B	144.	C	184.	A
25.	E	65.	E	105.	C	145.	A	185.	B
26.	D	66.	B	106.	C	146.	E	186.	A
27.	A	67.	D	107.	E	147.	C	187.	A
28.	E	68.	A	108.	A	148.	A	188.	D
29.	E	69.	C	109.	E	149.	D	189.	A
30.	B	70.	A	110.	E	150.	A	190.	A
31.	C	71.	B	111.	B	151.	E	191.	A
32.	E	72.	E	112.	E	152.	B	192.	E
33.	B	73.	B	113.	B	153.	E	193.	C
34.	A	74.	B	114.	E	154.	A	194.	B
35.	E	75.	A	115.	D	155.	C	195.	D
36.	B	76.	D	116.	C	156.	E	196.	B
37.	A	77.	A	117.	C	157.	B	197.	E
38.	D	78.	A	118.	C	158.	E	198.	C
39.	C	79.	E	119.	E	159.	B	199.	A
40.	D	80.	B	120.	A	160.	A	200.	D

SAMPLE TEST 1

EXPLANATORY ANSWERS

1. (D) On the retina is an insensitive area, the blind spot. Nerve fibers from the cells in the retina come together to form the bundle making the optic nerve. In the left eye, the blind spot falls to the left of the fovea, so that the area of blindness is in the left visual field; in the right eye it is on the opposite side.

2. (A) The cones are most "packed" in the center of the eye; as we go from the center of the retina to the periphery, the cones decrease in number. The cones connect through bipolar cells to individual optic fibers. Rods are active in night vision; cones are active in day vision.

3. (B) Pitch is a qualitative dimension of hearing correlated with the frequency of the sound waves that constitute the stimulus. Higher frequencies yield higher pitches.

4. (C) Recall is a technique of testing memory that requires the subject to repeat all that he has learned. Recognition just requires him to point out something he has seen or heard before. When the methods are compared, recognition scores are higher than recall scores.

5. (E) Tolman is a cognitive theorist; he did not believe, as do behaviorists, that learning consists of strengthening bonds between stimuli and responses. Rather, he believed that learning was a matter of developing a set of expectancies; reinforcement served to strengthen these expectancies.

6. (E) Teaching machines are based on the principles of operant conditioning; they are thus a direct application of the work of B. F. Skinner in operant conditioning.

7. (C) A sample is an estimate of the population or universe. Therefore, the mean of sample data must be an estimate of the mean of a universe or population.

8. (B) Karen Horney is a neo-Freudian personality theorist, placing greater stress on the social and ego development of man than did Freud. She is the author of the book Self-Analysis.

9. (C) The ego experiences moral anxiety as a result of warnings from the superego. Moral anxiety is one of three types of anxiety postulated by Freud; it is similar to neurotic anxiety, but not to realistic anxiety, in that the source of the anxiety is internal, not external.

10. (B) The Barker, Dembo and Lewin study was an experimental test of Lewin's theorizing about frustration (in terms of barriers to desired goals). Children, when frustrated, showed less constructive (regressive) behavior than they did when not frustrated.

11. (C) The memory trace is a hypothetical construct; that is, there is no such neurological entity discovered as yet, but the concept is a useful one in explaining phenomena of forgetting.

12. (B) Guthrie and his disciple Estes do not accept a decay theory of forgetting;

rather, they believe that new learning can cause "unlearning" of old learning. This process is generally called retroactive inhibition.

13. (E) Jung held that we all inherit a collective unconscious which is the same for all humans; he had also postulated the inheritance of the racial unconscious, which would be different among racial groups.

14. (B) An operational definition ties down the term being used to the processes used in creating it; an operational definition of hunger could be 24 hours of food deprivation, as an operational definition of thirst could be 24 hours of liquid deprivation.

15. (C) The most sophisticated scale is the ratio scale; it has an absolute zero point, and all the units are equidistant from each other.

16. (C) Nominal scales imply only differences in classification; they do not imply a continuum.

17. (B) The median just looks for the middle point in the distribution; the mean is the arithmetic average of all scores. Therefore, extreme scores are weighted into the mean, and will affect it much more than the median.

18. (E) The sensitivity of the eye goes from the violet end of the spectrum (about 400 millimicrons) to the red end of the spectrum (about 700 millimicrons).

19. (C) The method of constant stimuli pits several different stimuli against a standard; the subject has to say whether each of the stimuli is greater or less than the standard.

20. (B) In the method of limits, the experimenter varies the stimuli to be greater or less than the standard; the subject must say whether the stimulus the experimenter presents is larger or smaller than the standard. Order effects are particularly noticeable with this method.

21. (E) The International Candle has been adopted to measure the luminous intensity of a point source of light.

22. (A) If the distance from the source of light is 2 feet, the illuminance would be $(1/2)^2$.

23. (A) The pupil of the eye is constricted in bright light, and expanded (dilated) in dim light, in order to let in more or less light, as is required.

24. (E) The colors referred to here are called the additive primaries; in contrast to the subtractive primaries, when these additive primaries are added together, they produce white. Adding together the three subtractive primaries produces black.

25. (E) By examining the scatter diagram, the closeness of fit can be estimated without mathematical manipulation. However, the coefficient of correlation cannot be determined.

26. (D) Cones are responsible for color vision; the number of cones decreases to none as we go from the center of the eye to the periphery, while the rods (responsible for achromatic vision) increase as we go from the center to the periphery.

27. (A) The hypothesis of unconscious inference implies that sensations cannot in fact be observed but instead they are hidden, or overlaid, by unconsciously achieved conclusions.

28. (E) Osgood's semantic differential technique attempts to find the meaning of a word by having subjects measure where it lies in "semantic space": that is, where it lies along several bipolar adjective scales.

29. (E) Aphasia is an organically caused speech impairment. Hysteria, amnesia, dissociative reaction and fugue refer to different varieties of a psychoneurotic disorder classified under the general term dissociation.

30. (B) The Interpretation of Dreams was published in 1900; Freud's next publication was in 1904 (Psychopathology of Everyday Life).

31. (C) Breuer was also a Viennese physician; he taught Freud the benefits of the cathartic or "talking out your problems" form of therapy. The patient talked while the physician listened.

32. (E) The id represents our biological heritage; it is present at birth and unmodified by the passage of time or experience.

33. (B) The id derives its psychic energy through some transformations of bodily energy. The ego and the superego derive their energy from the id.

34. (A) It is the sole purpose of the id to create pleasure and dispel pain; pain is defined as the accumulation of tension; when tension accumulates, the id acts immediately to rid the person of the tension.

35. (E) Primary process is "wish-fulfillment"; it does not distinguish reality from fantasy, as does the secondary process. Primary process is a function of the id, while secondary process is a function of the ego.

36. (B) As stated above, wish-fullment, which does not distinguish reality from fantasy, is an example of the primary process.

37. (A) The mean is most often used to describe the status of a population in terms of a characteristic under study. This is because the distribution of data in many studies tends to form a normal curve. Observations in a normal study tend to center about the mean of the observations.

38. (D) The ego can distinguish reality from fantasy, while the id cannot do this, and makes no distinction between the real object and the mental representation of the object.

39. (C) Presbyopia is not a form of color blindness, while the other terms listed refer to color blindness.

40. (D) The aim of the reality principle is to postpone the discharge of energy until the actual object which will satisfy the need has been discovered or produced. In this way, the pleasure principle will be satisfied at the appropriate time.

41. (D) Both the ego and the superego derive their energy from the id; the id derives its energy from the bodily processes.

42. (E) Conscience is the internalized version of what the parent has punished the child for; the ego ideal is the internalized version of what the parent has rewarded the child for. The conscience punishes, and the ego ideal rewards.

43. (D) Empirical research has shown that the rods are most sensitive below 600 millimicrons, while the cones are more sensitive about 700 millimicrons. Rods are used for achromatic vision and cones are used for chromatic vision.

44. (A) Tests of significance or probability give estimates of the odds that observed results have been due to chance.

45. (B) The fovea is a small depression in the retina which is also the area of sharpest vision. The fovea contains only cones.

46. (C) The rods and cones are located toward the back of the retina. The center of the retina (the fovea) contains only cones and no rods.

47. (A) There are no rods in the foveal region of the eye; the cones provide all the visual acuity in that region.

48. (B) Empirical research has shown that we react more quickly to an auditory stimulus than to a visual stimulus.

49. (A) The data given has no bearing on the question. The abscissa of the standard normal curve is presented in

terms of standard deviations and the standard deviation at the mean, mode and median of the standard normal curve is 0.

50. (B) Maze learning shows the same phenomenon that learning a list of nonsense syllables does: mistakes drop out more easily from the beginning and the end than from the middle. This is called the serial position effect.

51. (C) Retroactive inhibition means that learning of the later task interferes with the recall of the task learned first. Proactive inhibition means that earlier learning makes later learning impossible.

52. (D) Retention curves are seen to drop off very rapidly in the first few hours after learning and then drop off more slowly with greater time between learning and testing.

53. (B) Student's "t" distribution is one technique used to handle the problem of small sample size in statistics. By definition, the sum of the square of deviations of sample observations about a sample mean is less than the sum of the squares of the deviation about any other point, including the population mean. Thus if the sample variance is used as an estimate of the population variance, the sample variance will be too small. In order to increase the estimate of the population variance, the sum of the deviations is divided by the number of the observations minus one rather than the sum of the observations alone. As the sample becomes larger, the difference in the variance caused by dividing by the number of observations minus one and the number of observations alone becomes small and Student's distribution approximates the normal distribution.

54. (A) Recognition memory has been found to be better than recall memory; this is due to the fact that many cues are provided to the subject in a recognition memory task, while he must supply all his own cues in a recall task.

55. (E) Wundt was a structuralist, who founded the first laboratory to study psychological (psychophysical) phenomena.

56. (C) Lashley's experiment indicated that the cerebral cortex plays a significant role in learning, since cortical removal impairs learning in direct proportion to the amount of cortex removed.

57. (B) Watson was the first behaviorist; he believed that only overt behavior was the legitimate subject matter of study for psychology. He did not use any constructs like images or sensations but described behavior in terms of implicit muscle movements.

58. (E) McDougall was primarily concerned with human instincts and propensities; propensities give rise to sentiments, and these in turn motivate adult behavior.

59. (B) The validity of a test cannot be greater than the square root of the reliability. Since .50 is the square root of .25, the test cannot have a greater validity than .50.

60. (C) The 1960 revision of the Stanford Binet allows for the computation of deviation IQ scores, so that a person can be placed relative to his age group. The previous method for determining IQ was to divide mental age by chronological age.

61. (B) The Terman and Ogden study indicates that children with superior IQ scores grow up to be superior adults, in both social and intellectual ways.

62. (D) The T-score system is a means of arriving at standardized scores. The mean of a test is set at 50, and the standard deviation at 10.

63. (A) The Z score is computed by subtracting the difference between the mean and the original score, and dividing this figure by the standard deviation of the distribution.

64. (D) In a normal distribution curve, 68.27 percent of the area under the curve falls between one standard deviation above the mean and one standard deviation below the mean.

65. (E) The term psychosis is usually applied when the individual is seen to have no contact with reality; the world of the psychotic is an hallucinatory world.

66. (B) The phobic person knows that there is no reason for his being afraid of what he is afraid of. On the other hand, the paranoic believes that he is being persecuted by forces which aim to destroy him.

67. (D) When the parent is too demanding, the child may stubbornly refuse to give his feces. If he elaborates on this childhood experience, he will mature into an obstinate adult.

68. (A) Psychometrics is used to determine the probability that observed differences between (or among) study groups are of a magnitude which might be expected to occur by chance.

69. (C) Guthrie believed that learning was one-trial--that is, all or none. Therefore, given the same stimuli, the animal should repeat its response exactly. The data from the experiment cited would give support to his theory.

70. (A) Guthrie held that the greater the degree of removal from the stimulus situation after the learning had occurred, the less possibility of interference of new learning with the old learning. He would therefore have argued that the reward changed the situation more for the animal than actual removal from the cage.

71. (B) A regression line has a least squares fit--that is, the difference between the observed points and the points on the regression line, when taken together, are equal to zero.

72. (E) The normal analogue of obsessive-compulsive neurosis is logical thought; obsessive compulsive thought is logical thought carried to a neurotic extreme.

73. (B) A negative reinforcer is some sort of aversive or unpleasant stimulation; its removal will strengthen an operant behavior.

74. (B) Hull had contended that exhaustion leads to extinction, while Guthrie's theory states that tolerance leads to extinction. The former is based on a reinforcement theory, the latter on a contiguity theory. Kimball and Kendall's data seem to support Guthrie.

75. (A) The punished response must be incompatible with some other response in the just punished situation. In this way, the latter response can take over, and the punished response will drop out of the behavior.

76. (D) Skinner feels that the explanation of language behavior in terms of <u>meaning</u> is superfluous. He feels that any and all behaviors, including language behavior, can be broken down into basic units of operant behavior and must be analyzed in these terms.

77. (A) Hull's theory is biologically based; he believes that all learning takes place inside the organism, and that all learning will eventually be explained biologically.

78. (A) Hull is a reinforcement learning theorist. In order to learn, there must be both habit strength and drive (motivation). The latter will be satisfied through reinforcement.

79. (E) Hull came to the final conclusion that practice in conjunction with reinforcement would systematically develop habit strength.

80. (B) Skinner believes that we should theorize only after much empirical work has been done; that is, we should draw conclusions from the data, rather than set out to test a hypothetico-deductive theory.

81. (D) Hull conceived of fractional anticipatory goals responses (which were intervening variables in his system) as serving both cue functions and reinforcing functions.

82. (D) Reactive inhibition is a natural concomitant of all responses; it will lead to fatigue and a diminution in learning ability, according to Hull.

83. (E) Skinner does not employ the concept of drive; he is concerned only with reinforcers, which are defined as anything that will strengthen the occurrence of operant behaviors.

84. (C) The psychopath is characterized by totally inappropriate social behavior. He lacks affect, and has no conscience about behavior which severely hurts others.

85. (A) A high correlation coefficient or coefficient of determination indicates that a mathematical relationship has been established, based on data that is generally historical in nature. Based on this mathematical relationship, it may be concluded that a cause and effect relationship may exist. For example, mathematically one could expect a high positive correlation between the present value of a privately-owned house as an independent variable, and the annual wage or salary of the owner, as a dependent variable. However, it would be imprudent to infer that the ownership of an expensive house would cause high personal income.

86. (C) According to Guthrie, the more motivated the organism, the more vigorous are his movements, and the more vigorous movement-produced stimuli they generate. Hence, there is a greater total number of stimuli which become attached to the learned response.

87. (B) Most behaviors are not just simple operants; rather, they are chains, in which one response may also serve as a certain kind of stimulus (say, discriminative stimulus) for the next response.

88. (C) Hue is color and depends on the wavelength of light; for example, the wavelength of 480m is blue and 573m is yellow.

89. (B) A reinforcer will strengthen the occurrence of some operant behavior, even when the operant behavior is totally accidental and "incorrect."

90. (C) The Tolman and Honzik experiment supports latent learning theory. This theory holds that learning is always taking place, but it will evidence itself only in the presence of reward.

91. (D) As the word "sample" is used in statistical terminology, it refers to a subject of a "population".

92. (D) According to Maslow, man is essentially born good; his development is determined by the degree of self-actualization that he subsequently achieves.

93. (E) Kretschmer had a two-fold classification of people based on bodily types: the lean and fragile type was called aesthenic, or leptosome, and the fat, rotund type was called pyknic.

94. (C) Angyal believed that man and his environment were totally interactive; he coined the expression "biosphere" to indicate this idea.

95. (A) A morpheme is a part of a word that is separable; that is, it expresses a particular function and is attached onto many different roots. In English, ed, ing, ous etc. are examples of morphemes.

96. (E) Moreno developed psychodrama, which involves the acting out on the stage of one's own life problems.

97. (D) Goldstein is a personality theorist who believes that man is motivated by a need for self-fulfillment, which he calls self-actualization.

98. (A) Idiographic studies focus on the study of the individual; they are like case studies.

99. (B) Allport and Vernon concluded that gesture was like a form of language for each subject; each subject was found to use distinct and stable gestures.

100. (B) Allport believes that mature motivations are functionally autonomous; that is, they are rooted in past biologies, but have come to function for their own sake, independent of any previous biological motivations.

101. (B) Functional autonomy refers to behaviors which now exist for their own sake, but had originated in the service of some biological need.

102. (A) Client-centered therapy is the creation of Carl Rogers. It differs from Freudian therapy in that it is less directive.

103. (B) Sullivan was a social personality theorist; he defined superstition as an instance of what he called "parataxic" experience.

104. (B) A discussion of additional research suggested by the results of a study may be of some interest and value, but it is not important to evaluation of the usefulness and validity of the report of the study itself.

105. (C) Henry Murray introduced the term personology; it referred to a personality theory focussing on the whole person.

106. (C) The mode is a measure of central tendency. It describes that value in the distribution which occurs most frequently.

107. (E) Any one of the listed factors can affect the results of a clinical study and throw doubt on or invalidate conclusions based on the results.

108. (A) Horney is a neo-Freudian ego psychologist. Most of her explanations of behavior are based on disturbances to ego functioning, rather than to sexual conflicts.

109. (E) Sampling must be random (and preferably stratified random) in order for us to know the true variability in the sample.

110. (E) A normal distribution has a single mode; a distribution with two modes is termed a bi-modal distribution.

111. (B) If the person must respond with one of a number of pre-selected alternatives, he is answering a fixed alternative question. If he is free to respond at length, the question is called open-ended.

112. (E) Murray developed the Thematic Apperception Test, which is a projective test based on the subject's response to a set of ambiguous photographs.

113. (B) In a distribution of n values, the n plus 1 value changes the mean by the (1/n plus 1) difference between itself and the mean. For example, if the mean of a distribution is 5, and the value of 10 is added, the new mean is 5 and 5/6.

114. (E) The probability function here is multiplicative: there is a probability of 1/4 on the first trial, and of 1/4 on the second trial; multiplying these probabilities gives a probability of 1/16 of both events happening.

115. (D) If a result is significant at the .001 level, it means that this result would happen by chance one out of one thousand times; a result significant at the .01 level means this result would happen by chance one out of one hundred times.

116. (C) The persona is the expected role; it is the mask man assumes to be acceptable in the eyes of society.

117. (C) Empirical evidence shows that upward mobility has remained constant in rate from the beginning of the Industrial Revolution to the present time.

118. (C) Relative deprivation theory is a sociological theory which states that satisfaction with outcome can be judged not only in terms of the absolute outcome, but that it should also be judged in terms of what the person's expectations for himself were, how well his peers did, and how difficult the task was, relative to reward.

119. (E) The social distance scale is supposedly a uni-dimensional scale; it asks how close you would allow another person to be to you. If a person is disallowed at some point (say, I would not allow him into my club), he should not be allowed to be any closer (allowed into the house, to marry my kin, etc.).

120. (A) The Authoritarian Personality attempted to find a psychoanalytically-based theory of ethnic intolerance and fascistic tendencies.

121. (D) "Stratified sampling" is a technique used to help ensure that different segments of the population are appropriately represented in selection of the sample.

122. (C) The reputational method of determining SES involves having people classify themselves and others in the status system. Objective methods involve techniques such as indices of occupation, education, and income per capita.

123. (A) Tryon's famous study has attempted to delineate where and how people in different social classes live.

124. (E) Pavlov's theory holds that if the conditioned stimulus is repeatedly paired with the unconditioned stimulus (if these stimuli are in contiguity), conditioning will occur.

125. (A) In color blindness, there is no sensitivity to hue if the color blindness is total. There is, however, sensitivity to brightness.

126. (B) Paranoid reactions are characterized by persistent systematic delusions. These delusions often take the form of delusions of grandeur or delusions of persecution. Paranoid symptoms are common in some types of schizophrenia, and most hospitalized cases with paranoid symptoms are classified as paranoid schizophrenics.

127. (E) The woman exhibited both delusions of grandeur and delusions of persecution; the paranoid diagnosis was based on these.

128. (E) Fear of water based on the idea that any water could drown one is a form of delusion of persecution; hence, the patient would be classifed as paranoid schizophrenic.

129. (B) Consistency is the term that best defines the concept of reliability. A test is considered to be reliable, if a person achieves consistent scores on both an identical retest of a test previously taken and on a test given with an equivalent form.

130. (A) The term "straight-line" is derived from the fact that a plotting of the correlations on graph paper forms a straight line.

131. (D) Criterion validity indicates the effectiveness of a test in predicting an individual's success or failure in certain criterion situations. The criteria might be subsequent job performance, grades in college, or mechanical problem-solving ability.

132. (A) In neurosis, the main victim is the patient himself. He wants desperately to be happy, but cannot. His fears, doubts and guilt feelings interfere with every aspect of his (or her) life.

133. (D) If overt behavior is the only legitimate subject matter for psychology, it follows that the non-overt states of conscious experience cannot be studied scientifically.

134. (A) Any insights that we can obtain into the behavior of any organism will contribute to psychology. Hence, animal behavior is a legitimate subject for study in and of itself.

135. (B) Objective functionalism studies the functions of behavior in an objective way; Watson studied in the functionalist tradition (which emphasized the function, rather than the contents of consciousness) and modified functionalism so that it was concerned with behavior, not consciousness.

136. (B) Behaviorists provide an experimental situation with carefully controlled stimuli, and observe the overt behaviors (responses) occurring in relation to the stimuli.

137. (D) The patient described evidenced both suspicion (the "fact" that the Communists were keeping his mail from

him) and grandiosity (his "cure" for cancer), thus making the diagnosis--paranoid schizophrenia, mixed type--applicable.

138. (C) Consummatory behavior is concerned with the physical act of satisfying some drive state. Eating and drinking are both consummatory behaviors.

139. (A) The amount of drinking rises rapidly for the initial periods of deprivation, and is less rapid as deprivation increases up to 48 hours. At 48 hours, the amount drunk will reach its peak; by 72 hours, it will drop off because of exhaustion and other factors.

140. (D) In order to control for associative strengths, the animals should be tested on the same schedule on which they were maintained. In this case, it is true that the results might have been contaminated by differences is associative strengths, but the results do show the group deprived longer ate more, and hence, had a stronger hunger drive.

141. (E) If subjects are familiar with all levels of deprivation, the observed relationship between motivation and extinction will not be contaminated by differing relationships in acquisition and extinction between the groups.

142. (D) Maze learning depends on differences in cues acquired in the mazes; cues are acquired as the animal is forced to both sides, or forced to rectify his errors.

143. (C) Miller and Dollard's model assumes (1) that the approach gradient is less steep than the avoidance gradient; (2) that at the outset, the approach tendency is greater than the avoidance tendency; (3) that the maximum conflict occurs where the approach and avoidance tendencies intersect; and (4) that increase in drive raises both approach and avoidance tendencies.

144. (C) As soon as the individual starts to move toward one goal, avoidance tendencies develop to the other goal (that is, relative avoidance tendencies; the non-preferred goal does not have a strong approach drive), and the conflict ends.

145. (A) Miller and Dollard's work is derived from the Hullian model, which is a pure stimulus-response reinforcement theory.

146. (E) Conflict will develop only when the tendency to approach is equal to the tendency to avoid. If one tendency is stronger, the animal will do that action without any conflict.

147. (C) Equity is a derivation from dissonance theory.

148. (A) The overcompensated pieceworkers are lowering their inputs to be more consistent with the outcome; in other words, they are reducing dissonance.

149. (D) Dissonance exists, and will be reduced when two cognitions or events are not consistent, but are in an obverse relationship to each other.

150. (A) Endomorphs are heavy people whose personality is dominated by visceral factors; mesomorphs are muscular types whose personality is dominated by muscular factors; and ectomorphs are thin people whose personality is dominated by cerebral factors.

151. (E) The suffix tonic, in Sheldon's terminology, refers to what part of the body dominates the personality. Hence, endomorphs are dominated by the viscera, and called viscerotonic, and ectomorphs are dominated by the cerebrum and called cerebrotonic; mesomorphs are called somatotonic.

152. (B) Somatotonia is characteristic of mesomorphs; they are dominated by the musculature, and hence, exhibit a strong need for muscular activity and physical exercise.

153. (E) Constitutional psychology has been concerned, to date, with the classification of people into personality types based on bodily build, and the interaction of biology with the environment. As far as processes such as the subconscious

are concerned, the constitutional psychologist would believe that they are related to biology, but he has not yet developed a theoretical position on the subject.

154. (A) The diagram shown is a model for a communications system. It is based on the model developed by Claude Shannon.

155. (C) Noise, or interference, is excluded. Noise enters all communication channels, so that input does not equal output, because it has been distorted by the noise in the communication channel.

156. (E) The source of behavior is the stimulus conditions; in an experimental paradigm, the behavior will be recorded by the observing psychologist, who is thus the "destination."

157. (B) The x axis is called the abscissa and the y axis is called the ordinate. The dependent variable is placed along the abscissa, and the independent variable is placed along the ordinate.

158. (E) When either of the two variables to be measured comes from a population with a narrow range (a homogeneous population), the size of the correlation is limited. The greater the spread in both samples, the larger the correlation can be.

159. (B) Drive is hypothesized to have both energizing and cue functions. As an energizer, it is a motivator of behavior. A drive also produces stimuli (S_d) which serve to channelize behavior, so as to satisfy the drive most efficiently.

160. (A) In order for a particular response to occur, there must be both drive (motivation) and knowledge of the behavior (habit strength). In a multiplicative relationship, both components are necessary; if either one is zero strength, no behavior occurs.

161. (D) Drive is an energizer of all behavior. In order for behavior to occur, in addition to motivation, the response must be in the organism's repertory (habit strength must be present).

162. (E) Secondary drives are generally learned (that is, they are not based on primary biological needs). These drives are not satisfied by objects such as food or water which would satisfy biologically-based or primary drives.

163. (D) Spence felt that in order for behavior to occur, habit strength, drive, and incentive must all be present; Hull stressed only drive and habit strength.

164. (A) Ability to form abstractions is the basic variable determing performance on concept formation tasks. Children, schizophrenics, and brain-damaged adults cannot effectively abstract; their thinking tends to be concrete, and they are poor at concept-formation tasks.

165. (D) Skinner is a learning theorist who has done work on operant conditioning and verbal conditioning. Hull and Hovland are both learning theorists who have worked in the area of concept formation; Hovland has applied an information theory model to concept formation.

166. (A) In order to arrive at the general, it is best that many instances of the specifics be presented. By seeing what the members of a class are, we can get more information about the class.

167. (C) When we want to correlate the rank orders of two bodies of data (say, rank in the class on math tests and on English tests), we use the Spearman rho. For non-ranked data, the Pearson product moment correlation technique is used.

168. (C) The just-noticeable difference is a barely perceptible change in the stimulus; it is a measure of the difference threshold.

169. (B) Two stimuli will be perceived as different if the difference between their magnitudes exceeds the "just noticeable difference" or j.n.d. The j.n.d. is determined by the relative magnitude of the stimuli and can be computed by the Weber-Fechner fraction.

170. (A) The independent variables are under the control of the experimenter; he varies these conditions systematically among experimental groups. Usually, the experimental group is subjected to some experimental variable of treatment, while the control group is not.

171. (D) Organic independent variables will deal with some bodily characteristic of the organism which is supposed to affect behavior. Force exerted on a lever would be a dependent variable (that which the psychologist would be measuring, not manipulating).

172. (C) Counterbalancing is done to insure that the variables themselves, and not the order in which they are presented, are affecting behavior. For example, if we wanted to test learning of abstract vs. concrete concepts, we would give half the subjects the abstract ones first, and the other half the concrete ones first, so that we would eliminate practice effects from the design.

173. (D) Heredity can be controlled in nonhuman populations through selective breeding; however, environment cannot be controlled because we cannot account for all the relevant factors in the environment, and we do not know what factors the organism considers relevant.

174. (D) Hebb, in common with most psychologists today, holds the view that heredity and environment interact, so that both are important. We should study effects on behavior of particular aspects of heredity and of environment instead of trying to solve the insoluble problem of which is more important.

175. (B) In the TAT, subjects are shown pictures of people, either alone or interacting; they are asked what is going on in these pictures. It is assumed that subjects will respond differently to the pictures, since they bring different personalities and different feeling states to the testing situation.

176. (D) In a sentence-completion projective test, there is no obvious one-word right answer. The test is geared to elicit some of the subject's feelings; hence, an item like "The aim of life is ...." would typically appear on a projective test.

177. (B) Rorschach scores are based on number of items seen, relationships between parts and whole of objects, color, form and movement. No separate category is made for reported conversations between stimuli on the cards.

178. (E) It is often said that a person's score on a projective test is due more to the personality of the scorer than to his own personality. This is a warranted criticism, since there are no standardized systems of interpretation, and since the score on a projective test is a qualitative impression rather than a quantitative measure.

179. (D) Tryon selectively bred maze bright and maze dull rats, so that after 7 generations there was no overlap between the two groups on maze-learning ability. When the rats were interbred, the offspring were mediocre in maze-learning ability.

180. (C) If attitudes have changed, the scores from before the message should differ from the scores after the message; therefore, the test will have low reliability, and will be sensitive to change in attitude.

181. (D) In regression, we predict the value of the unknown (y) from the known value of x. If y is seen to increase as x increases, then the relationship between x and y is linear and monotonic. (A curvillinear relationship would be non-monotonic: y would increase up to a certain value of x and then decrease again).

182. (E) Both the regression equation and the correlation coefficient indicate something about the relationship between two variables; however, correlation is not used for predicting, as is regression. Correlation can tell us only how variables are linearly related.

183. (E) The least squares method is the technique most frequently used for fitting a set of points (determining the

relationship between x and y). The least squares technique allows the x values to be chosen in advance, but not the y values.

184. (A) The regression fallacy refers to the fact that extreme scores tend to regress to the mean over time. Thus, extreme scores taken in January would probably be closer to the mean if these subjects were retested in June.

185. (B) The regression fallacy refers to the fact that extreme scores tend to regress to the mean. Another example of the operation of regression would be the tendency of very tall fathers to have somewhat shorter sons, and very short fathers to have somewhat taller sons.

186. (A) If the 12 men of the new tribe belong to tribe A (the population), then the mean head length of the population is 194 centimeters, as stated in the problem.

187. (A) When the original hypothesis is rejected, and this rejection is incorrect, a type I error has been made. If the original hypothesis is accepted when it is false, a type II error has been made.

188. (D) The problem presented here is a "textbook" problem; the investigator does not usually has as much information at his disposal as is given here, and he is usually not given such a simple task as selecting between two means. The problem is useful as an <u>example</u> of how we would go about testing hypotheses about populations.

189. (A) In this example, we would have to start by calculating the probabilities of making a type I or a type II error. We begin by finding the standard deviation of the mean of the samples. This would be equal to the standard deviation of the population by the square root of N: 8/ square root of 12.

190. (A) We assume a normal distribution of the populations in order to be able to determine the probability of making a type I or a type II error.

191. (A) Since most of the entries are piled up in the center of the distribution and fewer entries are in the ends of the distribution, the distribution approximates a normal one.

192. (E) Cumulative frequency curves are adding up the number of subjects as the magnitude of the intervals increase; non-cumulative curves just tell us how many subjects there are in each interval (cumulative curves tell how many there are in each interval <u>plus</u> all the intervals below that one). In plotting cumulative frequency curves, we use the upper limit of each interval, while we use the interval midpoint in plotting non-cumulative curves.

193. (C) Sublimation is a form of the defense mechanism of substitution, whereby socially unacceptable motives can find expression in socially acceptable forms. This is most commonly applied to the sublimation of sexual desires.

194. (B) Reaction formation is a defense mechanism in which the subject denies a disapproved motive through giving strong expression to its opposite.

195. (D) A defense mechanism is an adjustment made, often unconsciously, either through action or the avoidance of action in order to escape recognition by oneself of personal qualities or motives which cannot be reached, which may lower self-esteem or raise anxiety.

196. (B) Freud believed that there were two sources of man's basic instincts: the life force and the death force.

197. (E) Reliability can be ascertained through a coefficient of stability or a coefficient of equivalence. Giving the same subject the same test at different times is an example of the former, while giving the same subject similar tests at different times is an example of the later.

198. (C) A test may reliably measure performance of those scoring very high or very low on it, or those scoring in the middle ranges. If the test does not

adequately measure all ranges of ability, then it will not be reliable at all levels.

199. (A) A test is composed of a sample of items from the potential universe of items to measure the ability or trait in question. If we used all the possible items, then the test would be perfectly reliable. The longer the test, the closer it comes to including all possible items, and the more reliable it is.

200. (D) Construct validity is not concerned with predicting success at any particular criterion. Rather, the psychologist devises a theoretical construct which should be related to certain behaviors. He devises a test to measure this construct; if people scoring high on the test show behavior that people having a high degree of the construct should, then the test is said to have construct validity.

STEPS TO TAKE AFTER YOU FINISH SAMPLE TEST 1

STEP ONE—Now that you have taken the first Sample Test (under actual examination conditions, we hope), count the number of correct answers that you scored on the test. For each incorrect answer, deduct ¼ of a correct answer. This will yield your "raw score." What is your percentile ranking (refer to the table below)?

Before the Sample Tests in this book were approved for this publication, they were tried out by a generous sampling of students who were about to take the actual test. The results of this sampling provide the basis for this Percentile Ranking Table.

Although the Table is not official, it will give you a reasonably good idea of how you would stand with others taking the same test.

STEP TWO—You are urged to use the results of your first Sample Test in a scientifically diagnostic manner. Pinpoint the areas in which you show your greatest weakness. Do not be discouraged if you have done poorly on the first Sample Test. But do get to work immediately to eliminate your weaknesses.

STEP THREE—When you have strengthened yourself where necessary, take the second Sample Test. Again, place yourself under strict examination conditions. After you have taken the second Sample Test, go through the foregoing *Steps One* and *Two* just as you did after taking Sample Test 1. Repeat this procedure for the remaining sample tests. We have every confidence that you will do better and better as you take these Sample Tests provided you diligently and systematically follow the plan which we have outlined for you.

Now, please "get down to business" in getting rid of those "soft spots" revealed by your self-diagnosis of Sample Test 1.

Percentile Ranking Table

(Unofficial)

Approximate Percentile Ranking	Score* On Test	Approximate Percentile Ranking	Score* On Test	Approximate Percentile Ranking	Score* On Test	Approximate Percentile Ranking	Score* On Test
99	197-200	79	139-140	59	111-112	39	71-72
98	193-196	78	137-138	58	109-110	38	69-70
97	189-192	77	135-136	57	107-108	37	67-68
96	185-188	76	133-134	56	105-106	36	65-66
95	181-184	75	131-132	55	103-104	35	63-64
94	177-180	74	129-130	54	101-102	34	61-62
93	173-176	73	127-128	53	99-100	33	59-60
92	169-172	72	125-126	52	97-98	32	57-58
91	165-168	71	124	51	95-96	31	55-56
90	161-164	70	123	50	93-94	30	53-54
89	159-160	69	122	49	91-92	29	51-52
88	157-158	68	121	48	89-90	28	49-50
87	155-156	67	120	47	87-88	27	47-48
86	153-154	66	119	46	85-86	26	45-46
85	151-152	65	118	45	83-84	25	43-44
84	149-150	64	117	44	81-82	24	41-42
83	147-148	63	116	43	79-80	23	39-40
82	145-146	62	115	42	77-78	22	37-38
81	143-144	61	114	41	75-76	21	35-36
80	141-142	60	113	40	73-74	0-20	0-34

* After ¼ of a correct answer has been deducted for each incorrect answer.

TEAR OUT ALONG THIS LINE AND MARK YOUR ANSWERS AS INSTRUCTED IN THE TEXT.

ANSWER SHEET TEST (2)

1 A B C D E	35 A B C D E	68 A B C D E	101 A B C D E	134 A B C D E	167 A B C D E
2 A B C D E	36 A B C D E	69 A B C D E	102 A B C D E	135 A B C D E	168 A B C D E
3 A B C D E	37 A B C D E	70 A B C D E	103 A B C D E	136 A B C D E	169 A B C D E
4 A B C D E	38 A B C D E	71 A B C D E	104 A B C D E	137 A B C D E	170 A B C D E
5 A B C D E	39 A B C D E	72 A B C D E	105 A B C D E	138 A B C D E	171 A B C D E
6 A B C D E	40 A B C D E	73 A B C D E	106 A B C D E	139 A B C D E	172 A B C D E
7 A B C D E	41 A B C D E	74 A B C D E	107 A B C D E	140 A B C D E	173 A B C D E
8 A B C D E	42 A B C D E	75 A B C D E	108 A B C D E	141 A B C D E	174 A B C D E
9 A B C D E	43 A B C D E	76 A B C D E	109 A B C D E	142 A B C D E	175 A B C D E
10 A B C D E	44 A B C D E	77 A B C D E	110 A B C D E	143 A B C D E	176 A B C D E
11 A B C D E	45 A B C D E	78 A B C D E	111 A B C D E	144 A B C D E	177 A B C D E
12 A B C D E	46 A B C D E	79 A B C D E	112 A B C D E	145 A B C D E	178 A B C D E
13 A B C D E	47 A B C D E	80 A B C D E	113 A B C D E	146 A B C D E	179 A B C D E
14 A B C D E	48 A B C D E	81 A B C D E	114 A B C D E	147 A B C D E	180 A B C D E
15 A B C D E	49 A B C D E	82 A B C D E	115 A B C D E	148 A B C D E	181 A B C D E
16 A B C D E	50 A B C D E	83 A B C D E	116 A B C D E	149 A B C D E	182 A B C D E
17 A B C D E	51 A B C D E	84 A B C D E	117 A B C D E	150 A B C D E	183 A B C D E
18 A B C D E	52 A B C D E	85 A B C D E	118 A B C D E	151 A B C D E	184 A B C D E
19 A B C D E	53 A B C D E	86 A B C D E	119 A B C D E	152 A B C D E	185 A B C D E
20 A B C D E	54 A B C D E	87 A B C D E	120 A B C D E	153 A B C D E	186 A B C D E
21 A B C D E	55 A B C D E	88 A B C D E	121 A B C D E	154 A B C D E	187 A B C D E
22 A B C D E	56 A B C D E	89 A B C D E	122 A B C D E	155 A B C D E	188 A B C D E
23 A B C D E	57 A B C D E	90 A B C D E	123 A B C D E	156 A B C D E	189 A B C D E
24 A B C D E	58 A B C D E	91 A B C D E	124 A B C D E	157 A B C D E	190 A B C D E
25 A B C D E	59 A B C D E	92 A B C D E	125 A B C D E	158 A B C D E	191 A B C D E
26 A B C D E	60 A B C D E	93 A B C D E	126 A B C D E	159 A B C D E	192 A B C D E
27 A B C D E	61 A B C D E	94 A B C D E	127 A B C D E	160 A B C D E	193 A B C D E
28 A B C D E	62 A B C D E	95 A B C D E	128 A B C D E	161 A B C D E	194 A B C D E
29 A B C D E	63 A B C D E	96 A B C D E	129 A B C D E	162 A B C D E	195 A B C D E
30 A B C D E	64 A B C D E	97 A B C D E	130 A B C D E	163 A B C D E	196 A B C D E
31 A B C D E	65 A B C D E	98 A B C D E	131 A B C D E	164 A B C D E	197 A B C D E
32 A B C D E	66 A B C D E	99 A B C D E	132 A B C D E	165 A B C D E	198 A B C D E
33 A B C D E	67 A B C D E	100 A B C D E	133 A B C D E	166 A B C D E	199 A B C D E
34 A B C D E					200 A B C D E

GRE ADVANCED TEST IN PSYCHOLOGY

SAMPLE TEST 2

Time: 2 hours and 50 minutes

Directions: Select from the lettered choices that choice which best completes the statement or answers the question. Write the letter of your choice on the answer sheet.

1. The reality principle is obeyed by the

   A. id
   B. ego
   C. superego
   D. id, ego, and superego
   E. ego and superego

2. A researcher who worked on the isolation of single fibers of the gustatory nerve in animals was

   A. Pfaffman
   B. Robinson
   C. Koffka
   D. Hovland
   E. Hull

3. The main path of communication from the higher to the lower centers of coordination is the

   A. medical lemniscus
   B. column of Burdach
   C. lateral lemniscus
   D. spinal lemniscus
   E. pyramidal tract

4. The location of the "motor area" is in the

   A. precentral gyrus
   B. cuneas
   C. occipital lobe
   D. pons
   E. thalamus

5. The importance of the associative areas of the brain

   A. appears much greater with man than with the lower animals
   B. appears much greater with the lower animals than with man
   C. seems to be about the same with both man and the lower animals
   D. cannot be determined
   E. exists only for man

6. All tropisms are
   1. native rather than learned responses
   2. learned rather than native responses
   3. orienting responses to stimuli

   A. only 1 is correct
   B. only 2 is correct
   C. 2 and 3 are correct
   D. only 3 is correct
   E. 1 and 3 are correct

7. The correlation between the physical magnitude of the stimulus situation and the psychological interpretation of the magnitude is

   A. positive
   B. negative

C. sometimes positive, sometimes negative
D. practically impossible to determine
E. curvilinear

8. The wavelength of red is

A. greater than that of orange but less than that of blue
B. greater than that of blue but less than that of orange
C. greater than that of either blue or orange
D. less than that of either blue or orange
E. the same as the wavelength of orange

9. The Duplicity (Duplexity) Theory which states that the cones and rods make up two different functional types of retina receptors, was the result of data collected by

A. Young and Helmholtz
B. Katz
C. Hochberg
D. Newton
E. von Kries

10. An acceptable test must meet the following criteria:
1. discrimination
2. reliability
3. validity

A. 1 and 2 only
B. 1 and 3 only
C. 2 and 3 only
D. 1, 2, and 3
E. 2 only

11. Intelligence studies show conclusively that groups are to be ranked in this order (high to low):

A. professional groups, skilled workers, laborers
B. skilled workers, professional groups, laborers
C. laborers, skilled workers, professional groups
D. professional groups, laborers, skilled workers
E. skilled workers, laborers, professional groups

12. All of the following are measures of central tendencies except

A. arithmetic mean
B. geometric mean
C. medium
D. harmonic mean
E. variance

13. If an animal (such as a monkey or a rat) is placed on one side of an electrically charged grid, and an incentive is placed on the other side, you would likely find these results in order of drive-frequency:

A. maternal, hunger, exploration
B. exploration, hunger, maternal
C. hunger, maternal, exploration
D. hunger, exploration, maternal
E. maternal, exploration, hunger

14. The type of stimulation that determines the nature of a child's activity during the first few days of his existence is

A. proprioceptive
B. interoceptive
C. exteroceptive
D. none of the above
E. both A and C

15. The experiment in purposive behavior that Tolman conducted was one of

A. chickens pecking corn
B. children eating candy
C. lever-pressing by rats
D. hog-calling by farmers
E. maze-learning by rats

16. Another term for autistic thinking is

A. rationalizing
B. problem-solving
C. reasoning
D. daydreaming
E. perceptual defense

17. That learning is the formation of habit hierarchies was a theory expressed by

A. Hull
B. Tolman

C. Mendel
D. Otis
E. Spence

18. The stimulus that is most likely to bring about infantile fear is

A. a mouse
B. a shout
C. a fall
D. darkness
E. a slap

19. "The Measurement of Adult Intelligence" was written by

A. McDougall
B. James
C. Wechsler
D. Thorndike
E. Seashore

20. Paranoia is characterized by

A. psychomotor elation and depression
B. systematized delusions
C. loss of motive
D. deterioration of intelligence
E. incoherent speech

21. Which of the following statements would not be consonant with Adler's thinking?

A. All organs of the body strive independently for nutrition at some time before birth
B. At the time of birth, the organs begin to function together in accordance with the laws of compensation
C. The foundation of organic inferiority is psychic inferiority
D. Man can create his own personality
E. All life begins with feelings of superiority

22. Experimentation has revealed that following a shock of surprise, alarm, or the like,

A. the pulse rate decreases and the heartbeat amplitude increases
B. the pulse rate increases and the heartbeat amplitude decreases
C. both the pulse rate and the heartbeat amplitude increase
D. both the pulse rate and the heartbeat amplitude decrease
E. the pulse shows no change and the heart rate increases

23. Anosmia is the impairment of the

A. gustatory sensitivity
B. olfactory sensitivity
C. cutaneous sensitivity
D. sensitivity not listed above
E. hot-cold sensitivity

24. Overcompensation is indicated by the symptom of

A. depression
B. boasting
C. anxiety
D. malice
E. fixation

25. Psychic energy, according to Jung, is

A. id
B. ego
C. libido
D. phantasy
E. persona

26. "When a modifiable connection between a stimulus and a response is made and is followed or accompanied by a satisfying state of affairs, that connection's strength is increased. When that connection is made and accompanied by an annoying state of affairs, its strength is decreased." This basic principle was expressed by

A. Richter
B. Stratton
C. Thorndike
D. Reid
E. Guthrie

27. College entrance examinations originated with the work of

A. Russell
B. Yerkes
C. Otis
D. Cattell
E. Wechsler

28. McDougall's "Aspect Theory of Instinct and Emotion" is

    A. no longer given very serious consideration
    B. today given very serious consideration
    C. essentially in agreement with the Cannon-Bard Theory of Emotion
    D. essentially Freudian in its implications
    E. relevant to classical conditioning

29. Freud and his associates believed that, through motivated forgetting, events associated with a sense of guilt or shame

    A. could be remembered with treatment
    B. could not be forgotten in spite of treatment
    C. should be remembered for moral reasons
    D. should be recalled periodically for therapeutic reasons
    E. must not remain repressed

30. The probability of any event can be stated as some number ranging from

    A. 0 to 1, both included
    B. -2 to 2, both included
    C. 0 to 1
    D. -1 to 1
    E. any positive number

31. The experimental psychologist is indebted to Ebbinghaus for the latter's contribution in regard to methods for the study of

    A. animal emotions
    B. memorizing and retention
    C. mental differences
    D. drive and incentive
    E. reinforcement

32. Spearman is noted for essential ideas of

    A. personality dynamics
    B. factor analysis
    C. interpersonal relations
    D. psychological ecology
    E. concept formation

33. The "Biosocial Theory" was formulated by

    A. Jean Jacques Rousseau
    B. Gardner Murphy
    C. Kurt Goldstein
    D. Harry Stack Sullivan
    E. Karen Horney

34. A measurement technique employing correlation is

    A. paired comparison scaling
    B. equal interval scaling
    C. split half reliability
    D. successive interval scaling
    E. the scalogram technique

35. "A boundary which separates the stimuli eliciting one response from the stimuli eliciting a different response." This defines

    A. adjustment center
    B. conditioned reflex
    C. reaction time
    D. operant level
    E. threshold

36. All of the following are averages commonly used in treating educational data except

    A. mean
    B. mode
    C. median
    D. frequency
    E. both A and D

37. Of the following, the most useful for studying pupil-pupil relationships is the

    A. Rorschach Test
    B. Thematic Apperception Test
    C. Sociogram
    D. Anecdotal record
    E. MMPI

38. All of the following statements concerning standardized testing are true, except

    A. The operation of chance factors can bring about variations in scores

B. Individual tests are more likely to be valid in a given case than are group tests
C. The results of first-grade tests are likely to be invalid
D. I.Q. tests should be administered more than once during the K-6 years
E. The results of fifth grade tests are likely to be valid

39. Of the following concepts, the one least consonant with John Dewey's philosophy of education is

A. learning through experience
B. intrinsic motivation
C. emphasis on the learner rather than on the subject
D. democracy and pragmatism
E. extrinsic motivation

40. Of the following children with problems, the one most likely to have his problem overlooked in the classroom is the

A. retarded learner
B. habitual truant
C. aggressive pupil
D. shy, withdrawn pupil
E. passive pupil

41. Of the following abilities, the one which is least indicative of a child's readiness for reading is the following:

A. He speaks spontaneously
B. He has adequate vision, hearing and motor coordination
C. He has been taught the alphabet and many words at home
D. He has a satisfactory score on the reading readiness test and a mental age of about six and a half years
E. He speaks clearly

42. Left to right directional movement in reading

A. is natural to children
B. must be taught
C. is common to all cultures
D. has no connection with the reading process
E. occurs only in the Far East

43. "Correlation analysis" is a form of statistical testing which, in its simplest form, relates to studies

A. of the relation of one population factor and some one other factor
B. of the distribution of individual values around the mean of those values
C. in which two or more distributions of observations are compared directly
D. all of the above
E. none of the above

44. All of the following statements concerning social relationships in the early school years are usually true except

A. Groups are small and shift rapidly
B. Friends are selected because of propinquity and the accident of sharing objects
C. Children play and work with others to satisfy personal rather than social desires
D. Friends are selected on the basis of belonging to the same sex
E. Friends are not selected on the basis of sex

45. Of the following, the most valid reason for a teacher's making a case study of a pupil is to

A. learn more about education from the experience
B. discover the underlying motives for the pupil's behavior
C. develop an opportunity for telling him how to act more intelligently
D. find out what he was like as a young child
E. present the case to illustrate particular problems in teaching

46. Of the following, the American writer and teacher who has been most instrumental in furthering and interpreting the progressive movement in education is

A. Henry Barnard
B. G. Stanley Hall
C. Edward L. Thorndike
D. Margaret Mead
E. William H. Kilpatrick

47. All of the following statements about intelligence tests are true except:

A. Scores made by individual children may vary to a considerable degree over a period of time
B. There is a high correlation between I.Q. and academic aptitude
C. Current thinking holds that there are various kinds of intelligence in addition to the kind measured by paper and pencil group tests
D. "Culture-fair" I.Q. tests tend to favor the middle and upper socio-economic groups of our population
E. Current intelligence tests tap verbal intelligence

48. In New York State, according to a recent court decision, a pupil's I.Q. score

A. may not be given by the school to parents because of fear of misinterpretation
B. may be given to the child along with his reading score
C. must be given by the school to a parent who requests it
D. may be given to a parent upon the discretion of the principal
E. must be given to a child as a matter of course

49. All of the following are aspects of the readiness program before systematic instruction in reading is begun, except the

A. keeping of a bulletin board in the classroom with weather reports, special events, or messages to the children
B. labeling of objects in the classroom such as desks, chairs, and blackboard
C. use of a pre-primer as an introduction to a reading series
D. composing of little stories by the children which are recorded on a chart by the teacher
E. procedures in both A and D

50. Which one of the following educators is not noted for his work in the field of intelligence testing?

A. Louis Terman
B. Rudolph Pintner
C. David Wechsler
D. Robert Hutchins
E. Alfred Binet

51. The highest development of tests for observation and diagnosis are the

A. Binet tests
B. Goodenough Draw-a-Man Tests
C. Valentine Intelligence Tests
D. Seashore scales
E. Wechsler scales

52. A delayed conditioned response is easier
1. to set up than a simultaneous one
2. A trace conditioned response is more difficult to establish than either the delayed or the simultaneous one.

A. 1 is correct; 2 is incorrect
B. 1 is incorrect; 2 is correct
C. Both 1 and 2 are correct
D. Neither 1 nor 2 is correct
E. 1 is always correct; 2 is correct only for humans

53. Klüver and Lashley are known particularly for their work in

A. discrimination learning
B. vision and visual phenomena
C. distribution of individual differences
D. physiological drives
E. operant conditioning

54. Research studies demonstrate that <u>viscerotonia</u> correlates highest with

A. ectomorphy
B. endomorphy
C. mesomorphy
D. asthenia
E. dysplasia

55. The volley principle is an example of

A. reverberating circuits
B. temporal summation
C. ephapse
D. adaptation
E. Procion yellow

56. Studies of the intelligence of deaf and blind children have generally revealed

A. lower I.Q.'s among blind than among deaf children
B. lower I.Q.'s among deaf than among blind children
C. about the same degree of intellectual handicap among blind and deaf children
D. no handicap in intelligence test performance among blind or deaf children
E. superior I.Q. in deaf children and below average I.Q. in blind children

57. The largest proportion of mentally defective persons fall into the category of

A. undifferentiated amentia
B. mongolism
C. cretinism
D. microcephaly
E. hydrocephaly

58. According to the concept of the constancy of the I.Q., a child having an MA of 4 years when 5 years old will

A. have an I.Q. of 80 when 10 years old
B. will be of equal or better intelligence than 50% of a random population of his age level
C. be a mental defective at age 12 years 6 months
D. have an MA of 9 years when 10 years old
E. have an I.Q. of 120 when 10 years old

59. Identify the name or designation which is not appropriately grouped with the others.

A. schizophrenia
B. affective psychosis
C. manic-depressive psychosis
D. dycloid disorder
E. cyclothymia

60. The inability to express oneself in words in spite of an adequate understanding and imaginal representation is called

A. agraphia
B. aphasia
C. agnosia
D. aphexia
E. aphemia

61. If a known group of gifted children were given the 1937 Standford Binet and the Wechsler Intelligence Scale for Children (WISC), the WISC result as compared with the 1937 Stanford Binet result would be

A. lower
B. slightly higher
C. the same
D. unpredictably higher or lower
E. much higher

62. Of the following types of sub-tests present in the Wechsler-Bellevue Scales, the one which cannot be found in the 1937 Revision of the Stanford-Binet is

A. Picture completion
B. Digit span
C. Comprehension
D. Information
E. Both C and D

63. With regard to intellectual level and fluctuation of I.Q., Terman and Merrill maintain that

A. superior children show greater fluctuation in their I.Q.'s than do average children

B. superior children show smaller fluctuation in their I.Q.'s than do average children
C. dull children show greater fluctuation in their I.Q.'s than do average children
D. dull children show greater fluctuation in their I.Q.'s than do superior children
E. there is equal fluctuation in I.Q. shown by dull and superior children

64. When we continually present a conditioned stimulus with reinforcement, we are likely to produce

A. partial reinforcement
B. higher order conditioning
C. classical conditioning
D. operant extinction
E. experimental extinction

65. When an individual permits unpleasant impulses or thoughts access to consciousness but does not permit their normal elaboration in associative connection and in effect, the psychoanalytic adjustment mechanism involved is

A. rationalization
B. conversion
C. isolation
D. introjection
E. reaction formation

66. When it is said that an observed difference is significant at the one percent level, it means that

A. a difference as great as or greater than the one observed could be expected to occur purely by chance no more often than one time in a hundred
B. a difference as great as or greater than the one observed could be expected to occur purely by chance no more often than one time in a thousand
C. only one time in one hundred trials could something other than chance account for a difference as great as or greater than the one observed
D. only one time in one thousand trials could something other than chance account for a difference as great as or greater than the one observed
E. none of the above

67. Of the following personality mechanisms, the one that is an illustration of the fugue is

A. depersonalization
B. projection
C. regression
D. repression
E. introjection

68. The individual most prominently associated with the "birth trauma" theory is

A. Rank
B. Redl
C. Reik
D. Reich
E. Adler

69. Which one of the following represents an incorrect association?

A. Skinner - Operant Conditioning
B. Hull - Systematic Behavior Theory
C. Lewin - Field Theory
D. Thorndike - Connectionism
E. Guthrie - Sign Learning

70. In psychoanalytic thinking, repression can best be thought of as

A. an attempt in projection
B. a special type of introjection
C. a reflection of acceptance of Id impulses
D. a temporal form of regression
E. dominance of the ego by the id

71. According to the Freudian scheme of psychosexual development, which one of the following sequences is incorrect?

A. anal - phallic - latency
B. phallic - latency - genital
C. latency - phallic - genital
D. oral - anal - phallic
E. all are incorrect

72 According to classic psychoanalytic thinking, the disorder least responsive to psychoanalytic therapy is

A. compulsive neurosis
B. hysteria
C. narcissistic neurosis
D. obsessive neurosis
E. manic-depressive disorder

73. In Sullivan's thinking pre-adolescence is most frequently characterized by

A. heterosexual explorations
B. the development of intense chum relationships
C. the beginnings of realization of doctrination
D. the beginnings of realization of relative insignificance
E. homosexual exploration

74. Which one of the following is not intimately associated with the field of child therapy?

A. V. Axline
B. A. Freud
C. F. Fromm-Reichman
D. M. Klein
E. U. Bronfenbrenner

75. Piaget's concept of "ego-centric speech" refers to utterances by children

A. which are designed to influence the hearer favorably
B. who are self-absorbed and cannot talk about anybody but themselves
C. who do not place themselves at the point of view of the hearer and who consequently have but limited awareness of self
D. with marked and pathological autistic tendencies
E. with a high level of awareness

76. With respect to the possible use of scatter or pattern analysis on the Wechsler Scale as a basis for arriving at diagnoses of mental illness, the most nearly valid conclusions to be drawn from the results of most of the studies is that they

A. failed to support this use of scatter analysis
B. have given favorable support to this use of scatter analysis
C. demonstrated the validity of this procedure in the hands of well trained psychologists
D. demonstrated the validity of this procedure for most but not all forms of mental illness
E. distinguish clearly between normal and abnormal groups

77. Attention and concentration defects are best revealed on the Wechsler scales by failures on which of the following subtests?

A. Vocabulary and Information
B. Picture Arrangement and Comprehension
C. Similarities and Picture Completion
D. Object Assembly and Block Design
E. Arithmetic and Digit Span

78. Studies have shown that the average IQ of high school students is higher than that of elementary school students. The primary interpretation of this finding is that

A. high school students are better motivated than elementary school students to improve their intellectual standing
B. matured reading skills provide greater opportunities for intellectual growth in high school than in elementary school
C. intelligence test questions are more closely related to the high school curriculum than to the elementary school curriculum
D. the mentally and academically slow students tend to drop out of school sooner in their school career than above average students
E. none of the above is true

79. The manual of a new aptitude test to be used with children in grade 6 reported that the test correlated + .25 with the Stanford-Binet. Of the following, the best interpretation of this information is that the

A. aptitude test has low validity
B. aptitude test has low reliability
C. correlation coefficient was probably incorrectly computed
D. aptitude test questions are relatively independent of intellectual ability
E. aptitude test has high validity

80. It is preferable to compute the median rather than the mean of a distribution of scores when the

A. extreme scores would affect the average disproportionally
B. average having the highest reliability is desired
C. standard deviation is also needed
D. mean does not fall squarely on an integral value
E. data is taken from ratio scales

81. Which of the following criteria would not be used in appraising the content validity of a standardized achievement test in English for high school pupils?

A. Correlation of test scores with college English marks
B. Correspondence of the topics in the test with the topics covered in several English textbooks
C. Pooled judgment of a group of test experts
D. Agreement of the test items with a frequency count of errors in business letters
E. Pooled judgment of a group of writers of English textbooks

82. Under the normal curve, 95 percent of all observations fall between

A. 1 sigma and -1 sigma
B. 2 sigma and -2 sigma
C. 1.96 sigma and -1.96 sigma
D. 1.64 sigma and -1.64 sigma
E. 3 sigma and -3 sigma

83. From the reliability coefficient of a test one can judge

A. how consistently a person will maintain his position in the group if an equivalent test is given
B. how many points a person's score is likely to change if an equivalent test is given
C. whether or not the test is measuring what it is supposed to measure
D. whether or not the test is related to other significant traits within the individual
E. how well it can predict behavior

84. A research worker wishes to investigate the validity of a test battery for applicants to professional nursing schools. His most serious problem will probably be to

A. determine the objectives of nursing training
B. define a suitable criterion as a measure of job success
C. select the appropriate statistics to be used in the analysis of the test scores
D. gauge the appropriate length of each of the tests in the selection battery
E. examine all items in the test battery for face validity

85. Which choice is incorrect?

A. The Gestalt psychologists are not concerned about perception
B. Organic sensitivities are diffused feelings, seldom localized with any degree of exactness
C. The action of an organism upon its environment may be adaptive or nonadaptive
D. Learning occurs only at that time when the organism has attained an appropriate maturation level
E. Gestalt psychologists are interested in perceptual organizations

86. Defining personality as "the end product of our habit systems" expresses a concept most characteristic of a psychological orientation termed

A. structuralistic

B. psychoanalytic
C. Gestalt
D. personalistic
E. behavioristic

87. Control groups are important in clinical research as a means of

A. ensuring that samples selected for study are representative of the total population
B. enabling standardization of examiners to help ensure consistency of examiner results
C. providing a basis for comparison in evaluating the effectiveness of a test procedure
D. all of the above
E. none of the above

88. The effect of adding information to first impressions of personality is that judgment becomes

A. more accurate
B. less confident
C. confused with reduction in accuracy
D. less accurate
E. more confident but not necessarily more accurate

89. Studies on intelligence and creativity have yielded findings which indicate that

A. the two characteristics are completely independent
B. they are independent for subjects of high average ability and above
C. they are negatively correlated
D. for all practical purposes measuring one trait is essentially the same as measuring the other
E. the correlation is curvilinear

90. According to Freud's notion of an instinct, the most variable feature is the

A. aim
B. source
C. object
D. impetus
E. goal

91. According to Freudian concepts the displace-ability of energy early in life is due to the

A. flexibility of the ego structure
B. inability of the id to form fine discriminations between objects
C. immaturity of the perceptual process
D. operation of the super-ego
E. operation of the ego

92. Fromm's concept of the "marketing orientation" refers most immediately to

A. a person's aptitude for commerce
B. the undue value society places on competition
C. treating personal attributes and values as commodities
D. a person who is concerned with showing off
E. need for profit-making

93. Which theorist discusses modern man as being free from many of the restrictions of more primitive times, without having the freedom to develop himself fully?

A. Fromm
B. Kardiner
C. Horney
D. Sullivan
E. Rogers

94. What per cent of the scores in a distribution fall between the median and the third quartile?

A. 33
B. 50
C. 68
D. 75
E. 25

95. Laboratory studies of induced neuroses in animals show that

A. when the frustrating situations are removed, the animal's neurotic behavior disappears
B. animals have a lower tolerance than humans to frustrating situations

C. a single type of reaction to frustrating situations results
D. most induced neurotic behavior in animals is difficult to remove
E. all induced neurosis results in stereotyped behavior in the animal

96. Of the following, the psychologist who places least emphasis on practice as a factor in learning is

A. Thorndike
B. Skinner
C. Hull
D. Guthrie
E. Spence

97. Which one of the following is not a law of perception according to the Gestalt school?

A. proximity
B. similarity
C. good continuation
D. Pragnanz
E. readiness

98. The "median" may be more descriptive of a sample or of a population than is the "mean" in a situation where observations are

A. centered predominantly about two or more levels or centers of measurement
B. relatively evenly scattered about one level or center of measurement
C. characterized by a few relatively high or a few relatively low values
D. such that they form a bell-shaped curve when plotted in a frequency distribution
E. the number of subjects in the study is more than was needed for the sample

99. Maslow's theory of psychogenic needs in the human organism states that

A. during the elementary school years, social needs assume more importance than physiological needs
B. cognitive needs of the child emerge only with considerable stimulation in school
C. individual differences in strength of needs are so wide that any hierarchy of needs is meaningless
D. the hierarchy of needs remains constant throughout all of life
E. both C and D are true

100. A five year old is walking with his father and notes that there is a full moon. He says "Daddy, the moon is following us." What type of thinking is exemplified by the child's comment?

A. syncretism
B. perceptual defense
C. autism
D. primatism
E. animism

101. The process whereby an individual develops great sympathy towards another in order to conceal from himself certain malicious feelings toward this person, is known as

A. rationalization
B. intropunitiveness
C. extrapunitiveness
D. egocentrism
E. reaction formation

102. Paranoia is best understood in terms of the mechanism of

A. projection
B. regression
C. hostility
D. reaction formation
E. fixation

103. In hypothesis-testing, if the experimenter rejects a true hypothesis, he is committing

A. an alpha error
B. a beta error
C. a serious error
D. a forgivable error
E. a sigma error

104. Emotional reactions are so important in behavior disorders because they are

A. very intense
B. not readily changed from infancy to adulthood
C. difficult to communicate and share socially
D. so easily learned
E. hard to unlearn

105. The memory of an experience is most likely to be repressed when it is

A. unpleasant to basic senses
B. anxiety arousing
C. incapable of expression in fantasy
D. overstimulating
E. boring

106. The most basic requirement for the occurrence of projection is the presence of

A. underlying homosexual problems
B. underlying destructive impulses
C. an internal tendency judged to be unacceptable
D. a psychotic process
E. neurasthenia

107. Which of the following is not characteristic of the obsessive-compulsive defense syndrome?

A. regression
B. isolation
C. undoing
D. denial
E. repression

108. Repression maintains a phobia chiefly because it

A. is non-adjustive
B. changes the individual's personality
C. inhibits fear responses
D. impedes re-education
E. cannot be unlearned

109. Of the following, the information that a sociogram does not reveal is the

A. general pattern of group organization
B. network of group communication
C. reasons for choices and rejections
D. relative strength of choice status of individual members
E. number of two-way communications

110. In the course of taking the Rorschach, a client makes persistent efforts through selective perception and minimization to be conscious of only cheerful, pretty, innocent, sincere, untroubled, and otherwise positive aspects of experience. The examiner would be justified in suspecting the operation of the defense of

A. projection
B. denial
C. fixation
D. isolation
E. reaction formation

111. The psychologist who first proposed the concept of I.Q. was

A. Binet
B. Terman
C. Stern
D. Goddard
E. Wechsler

112. The "Guess Who" technique used in the elementary school is an example of which of the following?

A. self-report inventory
B. projective technique
C. sociometric device
D. problem solving test
E. concept formation test

113. Psychometric instruments for infants and pre-school children are best used for the

A. determination of the child's developmental status
B. prediction of the child's future intellectual status
C. understanding of the child's cognitive style
D. prediction of the child's potential for higher education

E. determining the child's I.Q.

114. Modern psychometric procedures tend to be characterized by their reliance upon

A. instruments utilizing ambiguous stimulus material
B. a differential approach to measuring abilities
C. general abilities instruments
D. psychologically pure single-dimensional scales
E. disguise and lack of structure

115. Of the following, the most significant reason for questioning the use of Wechsler's diagnostic score patterns is that

A. the subtests are not reliable enough
B. no plausible theory has been advanced to explain different patterns among psychiatric disorders
C. research has not shown significant differences between normal groups and abnormal diagnostic groups
D. subtests lack a defensible rationale about mental functions
E. not all subtests have predictive validity

116. While taking the Rorschach, a subject manifests naive verbalizations, unreflective responses, concreteness, literalness, and uses many cliches to express himself. The examiner would be justified in suspecting the operation of defense of

A. projection
B. denial
C. repression
D. regression
E. reaction formation

117. A teacher tells you that one of her students had difficulty solving a problem and made errors. Suddenly, he exclaimed he had the answer. It was the correct one. Of the following, the psychologist whose theory of learning would be most helpful to her in understanding the process her pupil underwent is

A. Skinner
B. Hull
C. Thorndike
D. Guthrie
E. Koffka

118. A student's score fell at the 80th percentile in a test of 50 items. This information tells the student that

A. he got 40 items correct on the examination
B. most of the class has higher grades than he
C. he exceeded 80 percent of his classmates in his test score
D. on an ordinary scale of grading he would receive the letter grade of "B"
E. 40 percent of the class did better than he did

119. The correlation between scores on tests of intelligence and achievement is

A. high and positive
B. low and positive
C. low and negative
D. inconsistenly variable
E. curvilinear

120. "A method of selecting a sample in which, after a random start, samples are made up by selecting on a systematic, periodic basis (such as every tenth child in a class)" is a definition of

A. cluster sampling
B. linear sampling
C. stratified sampling
D. ordered sampling
E. random sampling

121. A reliability coefficient based upon the split-half technique, when compared to a reliability coefficient derived from a retesting of the same subjects 6 months later, will usually be

A. higher
B. lower
C. just about the same as the second coefficient
D. higher or lower in accordance with chance
E. higher at the start - lower later

122. The correlation coefficient for which of the following pairs of measures would not be considered a reliability coefficient?

A. The results from two forms of the test administered to the same group at a single sitting
B. The results from the test and a criterion measure obtained from the same group at a single sitting
C. The results from two administrations of a test to the same group at different times
D. The results from two forms of the test administered to the same group at different times
D. Both A and D would not yield reliability quotients

123. If the reliability coefficient for a test based on group A is .85 and based on group B is, .45, we would expect that, if an equivalent test is given,

A. students will more nearly fall in the same order of performance in group A than group B
B. the ordering of students will be more nearly retained for group B
C. the average score for Group A will be higher than the average score for group B
D. the number of students above the norm in group A will exceed the number above the norm in group B
E. the average score for group B will be higher than that for group A

124. The Kuder-Richardson formula is used to

A. estimate the validity of a test
B. estimate the significance of the difference between two test scores
C. determine the reliability of a test
D. correct for the spuriously low odd-even reliability coefficient
E. determine constructive validity

125. The research procedure involving sorting of a series of statements into a group of piles approximating the shape of the normal curve is called

A. h sort
B. semantic differential
C. Likert type scale
D. Q sort
E. equal interval scaling

126. "A continuous distribution of observations in which, when plotted, the observations form a curve which is symmetrical about its mean" is a definition of

A. normal distribution
B. mean distribution
C. probability graph
D. ratio table
E. none of the above

127. The "Hawthorne effect" refers to the finding that

A. increasing the supply of light improves performance
B. special treatment incurred by virtue of being an experimental subject improves performance
C. performance can be improved only by improving the working environment
D. increased pay is the only effective way of improving performance
E. worker performance is optimal at 70° room temperature

128. Allport, in his personality theory, places major emphasis on

A. traits, but not on attitudes and intentions

B. traits and attitudes, but not on intentions
C. traits and intentions, but not on attitudes
D. traits, attitudes, and intentions
E. attitudes, but not on traits and attentions

Answer questions 129-130 with reference to the following data presented in graphical form.

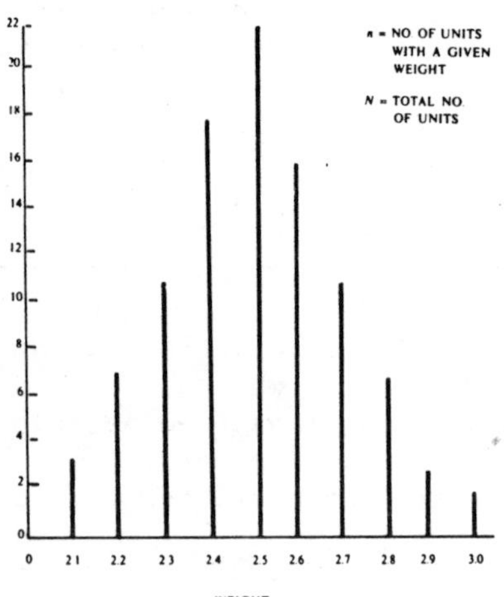

n	X	nX
3	2.1	6.3
7	2.2	15.4
11	2.3	25.3
18	2.4	43.2
22	2.5	55.0
16	2.6	41.6
11	2.7	29.7
7	2.8	19.6
3	2.9	8.7
2	3.0	6.0

129. The root mean square deviation(s) for such a set of data is given by

A. $[\frac{1}{N - 1} \Sigma n(X - X_{avg})\ ]^{1/2}$

B. $[\frac{1}{N - 1} \Sigma (X - X_{avg})^2]$

C. $[\frac{1}{N - 1} \Sigma n(X - X_{avg})^2]^{1/2}$

D. $[\frac{1}{N - 1} \Sigma (X - X_{avg})]^{1/2}$

E. $[\frac{1}{N - 1} \Sigma (X - X_{avg})^3]^{1/2}$

130. The value of s is closest to which of the following if X_{avg} is taken as 2.50?

A. 0.04
B. 0.40
C. 0.06
D. 0.63
E. 0.20

Answer questions 131-135 with reference to the following curves:

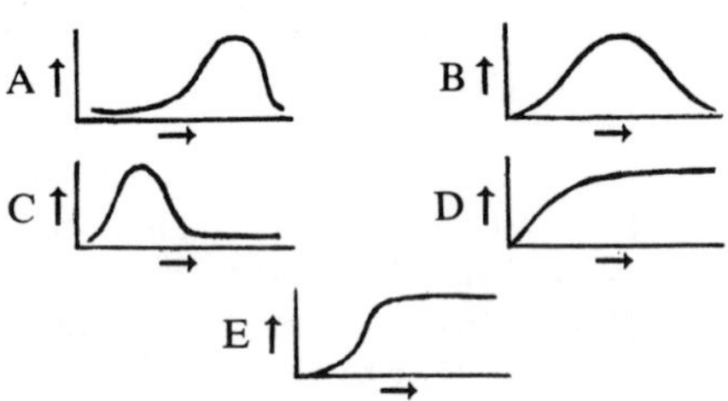

Choose the curve, A, B, C, D, or E to which each of the following statements best applies:

131. The distribution of heights in a representative random sample of male adults

132. The mean, median and mode are equal

133. The idealized learning curve

134. An ogive

135. The curve which discriminates least well among students scoring high on a test

Answer questions 136-140 with reference to the passage quoted below.

Sensory stimuli such as air vibration and light and chemical aspects of the environment initiate messages which are carried to the brain after being received by the sense receptors. These messages are decoded by the brain; they are carried to the brain and away from it by nerve fibers. Physiological psychologists are concerned with studying both the similarities and the differences between different kinds of sensory input and sensory output.

136. All the following are parts of a neuron except

A. the cell body
B. axons
C. dendrites
D. plasma
E. both C and D

137. When a physiological psychologist is studying a motor-effector neuron, he is studying

A. an afferent neuron
B. an efferent neuron
C. neuilemma
D. spinal nerves
E. none of the above

138. If a physiological psychologist stimulates a particular neuron, the period immediately after stimulation and activation is called

A. the absolute refractory period
B. relative refractory period
C. reflective period
D. resting state
E. the frequency of discharge in each fiber of the optic nerve stays constant

139. All messages from auditory receptors will end up

A. in the thalamus
B. in the medulla
C. in different (unspecifiable) parts of the cerebral cortex
D. in a designated auditory area in the cortex
E. in the cerebellum

140. Nerve fibers in the central nervous systems are "connected" via

A. synapses
B. neurilemma
C. myelin
D. connective tissue
E. none of the above

Answer questions 141-142 with reference to the passage quoted below.

Psychology must study scientifically the behavior of organisms. Therefore the field of animal behavior is legitimately included in the field of psychology. We can no sooner infer consciousness from the behavior of animals than we can from the behavior of humans. The same methods used to study animal behavior can be used to study human behavior. The psychologist studying human behavior, just as the psychologist studying animal behavior, can have no access to the consciousness of the subject, and therefore cannot scientifically infer consciousness from his experimental observations or data.

141. This point of view holds that

A. conscious experience does not exist
B. introspective reports should be taken as descriptions of conscious experience
C. introspective reports are objective
D. conscious experience cannot be studied scientifically
E. both A and D are true

142. A psychologist expressing the view given in the paragraph holds that

A. animal behavior is a valid subject for study in its own right
B. animal behavior should be studied to gain information about animal consciousness
C. animal behavior should be studied only to develop methods for studying human behavior
D. animal behavior should be studied because of the light it sheds on human behavior
E. animal behavior should be studied in preference to human behavior

Answer questions 143-149 with reference to the passage quoted below.

Some experimental animals are placed in an apparatus. They emit many of the possible responses in their repertory. One response, that of pressing a lever, has been selected by the experimenter to be reinforced by food. One group of animals is rewarded with a pellet of food every 10th time that one of this group presses the lever (Group A). The other group of animals (Group B) is rewarded with a pellet of food at 5 minute intervals, regardless of the number of bar presses made within that period of time.

143. The responses which are reinforced in this experimental situation are described most exactly as:

A. reinforced responses
B. conditioned responses
C. operants
D. unconditioned responses
E. elicited responses

144. The experimental schedules described above are called, for group A and group B respectively,

A. fixed ratio and fixed interval
B. fixed interval and fixed ratio
C. variable interval and fixed ratio
D. variable ratio and variable interval
E. variable ratio and fixed interval

145. In instrumental conditioning, as described above,

A. the reinforcer is paired with a stimulus
B. the reinforcer is paired with a response emitted by the subject
C. the reinforcer is paired with a discriminative stimulus
D. the reinforcer is paired with a response elicited from the subject
E. both A and C are true

146. Typical curves for fixed ratio reinforcement show

A. an invariably high rate of responding
B. a slow rate of responding after each reinforcement
C. a high rate of responding if the animal need not work too long for another reinforcement to occur
D. a uniformly slow rate of responding
E. no predictable relationship between reinforcement and response

147. The psychologist responsible for development of the above methodology is

A. Skinner
B. Pavlov
C. Hull
D. Estes
E. Guthrie

148. The click of the lever, associated with the presentation of the pellet, works as

A. a primary reinforcer
B. a secondary reinforcer
C. a discriminative stimulus
D. both A and C
E. both B and C

149. Variable ratio reinforcement schedules are most like the "real-life" situation of

A. finishing a job on a tight schedule
B. having 'piece-work' employment
C. gambling
D. learning to accept any one of several possible choices as reinforcers
E. learning opposed skills simultaneously

150. Analysis of Variance measures observed effects against the null hypothesis and ultimately yield a variance ratio whose value is identified by the term

A. t
B. F

C. Z
D. Chi square
E. Baysian

Answer questions 151-155 with reference to the passage quoted below.

Psychologists recently conducted an important experiment dealing with the emotions. All subjects were given an injection of adrenalin. Immediately following this injection, they were placed in a room with either an angry or a euphoric "stooge." Half of the subjects had been told that the injection would create symptoms that it did; the other half expected no physiological effect of the injection. This latter half was found to become angry (when with the angry stooge) or euphoric (when with the euphoric stooge) with far greater intensity than the group which was informed as to the effects of the injection. On the basis of this and several other experiments, psychologists concluded that the emotion is a joint function of cognitive and physiological experience.

151. The experiment described above has shown that

A. emotions are entirely dependent on the visceral state produced
B. different emotions can arise from the same visceral state
C. visceral arousal is not necessary for corresponding emotional arousal
D. given a state of physiological arousal, the emotions shown will depend on available cognitions
E. both B and D are true

152. These experiments support the James-Lange theory of emotion in that they show

A. emotions are merely perception of visceral reactions
B. visceral conditions are necessary for emotional events to occur
C. different emotions come from different patterns of visceral arousal
D. both A and C are true
E. both B and C are true

153. Cannon offered all of the following criticisms of the James-Lange theory of emotion except that

A. Emotional behavior may be present when the sympathetic nervous system is not intact
B. Visceral changes differ from emotion to emotion
C. The viscera are insensitive, and visceral feedback is too indistinct to provide adequate information
D. Visceral changes are too slow to produce immediate emotion
E. Artificial production of visceral changes (by drugs) does not induce emotion

154. If a subject in an experiment similar to the above were to receive an injection of adrenalin, be misinformed as to its effects, and be placed in a room with an angry stooge, we would expect his emotionality, relative to the other groups, to be

A. more emotional than both the informed and uninformed
B. less emotional than both the informed and uninformed
C. more emotional than the informed, but less than the uninformed
D. more emotional than the uninformed but less than the informed
E. unpredictable since the theory is not able to predict for this condition

155. If we had the same three conditions as in the previous question, but now, half the subjects in each condition were given a placebo rather than adrenalin, we would predict that

A. the ordering is entirely dependent on the information given, not on whether he has a placebo or adrenalin
B. no placebo subjects would show emotion
C. placebo subjects would show emotion only insofar as they

were self-aroused by the injection
D. only ignorant or misinformed subjects will show emotion, in both the placebo and the adrenalin condition
E. both B and C will be true

156. Regression Analysis is primarily a(an)

A. estimating device
B. statistic
C. parameter
D. graph
E. self-sustaining analysis

Answer questions 157-160 with reference to the passage quoted below.

The "hard" sciences of physics and chemistry have provided a great influence in certain areas of psychology; they have provided psychologists with new and often fruitful ways of thinking about the phenomena of personality and behavior. For example, the "field theory" of physics, derived from the 19th century work of the physicists Faraday and Maxwell, has provided strong impetus for 20th century psychological theorizing. In particular, there has been the work of Kurt Lewin. To Lewin, the field in which behavior occurs refers to the totality of existing psychological facts, which, at any given time, are interdependent. Behavior is a function of this field, and analysis of behavior begins with analysis of the situation as a whole. Within the field, behavior is determined by forces such as tension and energy; the object is to return the field to a state of equilibrium.

157. In general, a field theoretical approach would hold that

A. fixed, absolute characteristics of the individual components of the field are the important determinants of subsequent perception or behavior
B. the way in which an object affects perception or behavior is determined by the configuration of the whole in which the object is imbedded
C. relationships between various components in the field are the important determinants of subsequent perception or behavior
D. all of the above are true
E. B and C are true

158. According to Lewin, psychological disequilibrium exists when there is unequal tension in various of the systems in the life space. It is possible for the person to restore equilibrium by

A. performing a direct locomotion which will bring the person into the range of a satisfying goal object
B. performing a substitute locomotion; that is, satisfying one need to relieve the tension of a related need system
C. performing vicarious locomotions such as daydreaming
D. all of the above
E. none of the above

159. Lewin believed that the person in any given situation could be represented mathematically. In order to do so, he used

A. Euclidian space
B. a finite probability model
C. hodological space
D. a multiplicative algebraic model
E. an additive algebraic model

160. As the adult develops, Lewin holds that certain psychological changes occur. Which of the following statements are not true:

A. With maturity, the number of regions in the life space become increasingly differentiated
B. Various tension systems become interdependent
C. There is no change in the boundaries between systems with maturity
D. It will generally be easier for children than for adults to substitute one need for another
E. Maturation is accompanied by

the establishment of hierarchy of dominant-subordinate need systems

161. In a clinical study

A. the type of data to be collected should be determined in the planning stage and the method of data management should be determined early in the evaluation stage
B. the type of data to be collected and the method of managing the data should both be considered early in the planning stages of the study
C. the type of data to be collected and the method of managing the data cannot be determined until after the sample and the index (es) to be used have been studied
D. A and C answers
E. none of the above

Answer questions 162-166 with reference to the passage quoted below.

If we wish to understand what happens when a skill is learned, we must concern ourselves with individual movements, rather than with the end act that is performed or the goal which is achieved. When a complex skill appears to be learned only gradually, it is important to remember that this seemingly slow learning is due to the fact that each skill is composed of many movements, each of which must be learned and attached to the proper cues. The actual learning of any given movement is accomplished in one trial; some combination of stimuli which has accompanied a movement will tend, on its recurrence, to be accompanied again by that movement.

162. The above statement represents the theoretical position of

A. Tolman
B. Hebb
C. Hull
D. Guthrie
E. Skinner

163. The paragraph indicates that the time relationship between cue and response

A. is not relevant to learning
B. must be strictly simultaneous; it is movement-produced stimuli that become conditioned to the movement
C. is best for learning if the cue occurs 30 seconds or less before the response
D. cannot truly be measured because the psychologist does not have direct control over the movement-produced stimuli
E. applies to both B and D

164. The paragraph holds that

A. learning occurs only with adequate reinforcement
B. learning requires a clearly visible goal
C. learning requires many repetitions of a single response to stamp in that response
D. all learning is one trial
E. all learning is contingent on underlying motivations

165. The theory considers the important dependent variable

A. success of the organism in reaching a goal
B. rate of learning to reach a goal
C. number of errors in reaching a goal
D. movements of the organism
E. speed in reaching the goal

166. The theory of learning expressed in the following paragraph would predict

A. that the subject will tend to repeat its behavior exactly, given an identical stimulus situation
B. that the subject will be able to reach the same goal, given an identical stimulus situation
C. behavior is identical with similar stimulus situations

D. both B and C
E. none of the above

167. All of the following are part of the limbic system except:

A. amygdala
B. hypothalamus
C. thalamus
D. septum
E. cerebellum

168. Identify the name or designation which is not appropriately grouped with the others.

A. renonance theory
B. dissonance theory
C. frequency theory
D. volley-place theory
E. Von Bekesy's theory

Answer questions 169-171 with reference to the passage quoted below.

Learning theory is generally said to be divided into stimulus-response and cognitive theories. While cleavages at first appear sharp, many of the distinctions later blur; all theorists accept data which has been soundly gathered, and as more data is collected, a higher level of commonly accepted relationships begins to emerge. What seem to be diametrically opposed points of view, then, may be differences in preference. Certain issues of contention - contiguity vs. reinforcement, types of learning, and kinds of theoretical mediators used - cut across the traditional stimulus-response vs. cognitive dichotomy.

169. One way in which the stimulus-response theorist differs from the cognitive theorist is that

A. stimulus-response theorists prefer to find movement intermediaries as integrators of behavior sequences
B. stimulus-response theorists prefer to use central brain processes as integrators of behavior sequences
C. stimulus-response theories do not use intermediaries which must be inferred from behavior
D. both A and C
E. both B and C

170. A stimulus-response psychologist and a cognitivist who both accept the notion that learning occurs by contiguity are

A. Guthrie and Tolman
B. Hull and Tolman
C. Guthrie and Hebb
D. Hull and Skinner
E. Hull and Festinger

171. An intermediary variable which need have no surplus meanings other than those expressed in its units of measurement is called

A. an intervening variable
B. a hypothetical construct
C. an organismic variable
D. an intervening-dependent variable
E. a postulate

172. The method of correlation for ranked data is

A. Pearson product moment correlation
B. Kendall's tau
C. Spearman's rho
D. Kendall's zeta
E. multiple correlation

173. A fasciculus differs from a tract because it possesses a different

A. function
B. point of termination
C. point of origin
D. position in the spinal cord
E. position in the peripheral nervous system

Answer questions 174-178 with reference to the passage quoted below.

A person is in need of psychotherapy when, because of the by-products of excessive control of others in his personal behavior history, he cannot function properly or becomes dangerous to himself. What is wrong about his functioning or what is dangerous about his actions must be determined by examining the consequences of his actions. It is the job of the therapist to change or add to the personal behavior history of the patient so that the patient's behavior no longer displays these characteristics of malfunctioning and danger.

174. It is the job of psychotherapy, according to the above view, to

A. redirect behavior along healthier lines
B. examine id-ego-superego conflicts which impede functioning
C. effect transference so that behavior can be redirected
D. have the person understand his own conflicts
E. have the person understand why his actions are potentially dangerous

175. The type of psychotherapy described above is supported by

A. Sullivan
B. Horney
C. Adler
D. Skinner
E. Jung

176. According to the above point of view, a therapist dealing with a phobic disorder should

A. concentrate on getting at the underlying causes of the phobia
B. first learn the dynamics of the phobia
C. try to rid the patient of the symptom
D. do both A and B
E. do none of the above

177. A concept most likely to be acceptable to a psychologist holding the point of view expressed above is

A. libido
B. shaping up
C. transference
D. collective unconscious
E. need for personal autonomy

178. A recent experiment by a group of psychologists holding this point of view has attempting to treat mental patients by

A. structured group therapy sessions
B. electric shock
C. reinforcement with cigarettes for responses desired by the experimenters
D. punishment with noxious stimulation for undesirable responses
E. both B and D

179. Lesions in the thalamus universally cause

A. disequilibrium
B. sensory impairment at the level of acuity
C. prolonged wakefulness
D. intractable pain
E. hunger

180. When observations form a "normal" distribution about their mean, approximately what percent of the observations fall within two standard deviations, above, and two standard deviations below the mean?

A. 34 percent
B. 50 percent
C. 67 percent
D. 95 percent
E. 98 percent

Answer questions 181-184 with reference to the illustration below.

USC (food) →
CS (bell) → CR (salivation)

181. Classical conditioning does not involve

A. reward
B. escape from pain
C. avoidance of pain
D. any of the above
E. either A or C

182. The term conditioned response refers to a response that

A. is elicited by the unconditioned stimulus before and after conditioning

B. is elicited by the unconditioned stimulus only after conditioning
C. is elicited by the previously neutral stimulus (CS) after conditioning
D. acts as described in both A and C
E. acts as described in both B and C

183. Classical conditioning is thought by Skinner to involve

A. striated muscle
B. smooth muscle
C. epi-gastric secretion
D. neuro-hormonal secretion
E. voluntary muscle

184. Backward conditioning refers to

A. the presentation of the CS before the UCS
B. simultaneous presentation of the CS and UCS
C. attempting to condition a response that does not originally exist to the UCS
D. presentation of the UCS before the CS
E. presentation of the CS at least 5 minutes after the UCS

185. The influence or accessibility of one region to another, and the ability of a person to move from one region to another is called by Lewin

A. locomotion
B. flexibility
C. absorption
D. interreliance
E. communication

Answer questions 186-189 with reference to the passage quoted below.

Psychology may be said to be the study of consciousness. The existential psychologist is interested in discovering the elements of consciousness, rather than how consciousness operates on the world. To find the elements of consciousness, the experience of the Observer must be analyzed into the irreducible minimum, stripped of everyday meaning.

186. The point of view represented in the above paragraph is that of the

A. Gestalt school
B. Freudian school
C. Structuralist school
D. Functionalist school
E. Behaviorist school

187. The functionalist school of psychology differed from the structuralist in

A. functionists opposed the use of introspection
B. functionalism did not regard consciousness as the proper study of psychology
C. functionalists maintained the importance of studying the operations of consciousness as part of the organism's biological adaptation to his environment
D. structuralists felt that consciousness was only an epiphenomenon
E. both A and B

188. Structuralists studied all the following except

A. sensations
B. images
C. perceptions
D. reflexes
E. feelings

189. The Observer mentioned in the foregoing paragraph would most likely be

A. the person recording the behavior of the subject
B. the subject giving introspective reports of his own experience
C. the person examining the interaction between the subject and the experimenter
D. the person reporting overt behavioral changes during an experiment (on the part of the subject)
E. none of the above

190. "That portion of a population affected by a disease or other condition at a given time," is a definition of

A. incidence
B. frequency
C. prevalence
D. sample
E. dependent variable

Answer questions 191-195 with reference to the passage quoted below.

It is fairly frequent in psychological experiments that the experimenter is forced to admit that he has no knowledge of what the statistical distribution of the variable he is studying is like. A problem also frequently arises insofar as the experimenter knows that the variable he is studying does not meet the requisites for the application of the desired statistical procedure. For example, he may know that the distribution of a variable is not normal, but he still may be interested in testing whether the mean of such a distribution has a specified value. To circumvent these difficulties, statistical procedures called non-parametric tests have been developed.

191. According to the above paragraph, non-parametric tests are used

A. for normal distribution only
B. in situations where the mean is not determined
C. where the variable does not meet the assumptions required by standard tests
D. in any of the above situations
E. in none of the above situations

192. All of the following are non-parametric methods except

A. sign test
B. analysis of variance
C. rank-sum test
D. rank correlation coefficient
E. both B and D

193. Non-parametric problems relating to continuous variables differ from the standard parametric ones in that the former is more likely to

A. use the mean as the measure of location of the distribution
B. use the median as the measure of location of the distribution
C. use the mode as the measure of location of the distribution
D. use no measure of central tendency
E. act in the way described in both B and C

194. If we wish to test the difference of two medians non-parametrically, we use

A. chi-square
B. analysis of covariance
C. student's t-test
D. rank-sum test
E. rank correlation coefficient

195. Non-parametric methods will have to be used to determine the extent of linear relationships between two variables if these variables are

A. not normally distributed
B. not both discrete
C. not both continuous
D. both A and C
E. internal measures

196. Non-parametric methods will not be used if the data can fit which of the following systems of measurement?

A. ordinal
B. nominal
C. interval
D. ratio
E. both C and D

Answer questions 197-200 with reference to the figures below.

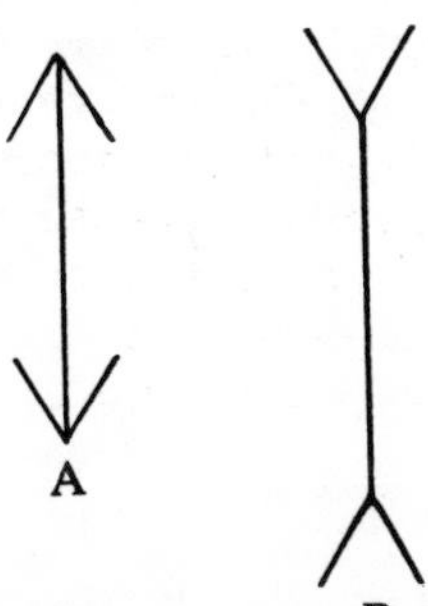

197. The figures shown above are called

   A. the contextual illusion
   B. the Gibson illusion
   C. the Muller-Lyer illusion
   D. the phi-phenomenon
   E. the Weber-Fechner illusion

198. The above figures constitute an illusion because

   A. they belie size constancy
   B. they distort depth cues
   C. we preceive the lines as being of different length
   D. both A and C are true
   E. both B and C are true

199. Other examples of a disparity between proximal stimulation and appearance are

   A. light constancy
   B. size constancy
   C. organizational effects
   D. A and B
   E. A, B, and C

200. The observing of motion without accompanying successive retinal stimulation is called

   A. the phi-phenomenon
   B. motion constancy
   C. the law of organized stimuli
   D. the camouflage effect
   E. none of the above

SAMPLE TEST 2

ANSWER KEY

1.	B	41.	C	81.	A	121.	A	161.	B
2.	A	42.	B	82.	C	122.	B	162.	D
3.	E	43.	A	83.	A	123.	A	163.	E
4.	A	44.	D	84.	B	124.	D	164.	D
5.	A	45.	B	85.	A	125.	D	165.	D
6.	E	46.	E	86.	E	126.	A	166.	A
7.	A	47.	D	87.	C	127.	B	167.	E
8.	C	48.	C	88.	E	128.	D	168.	B
9.	E	49.	A	89.	B	129.	C	169.	A
10.	D	50.	D	90.	C	130.	E	170.	A
11.	A	51.	E	91.	C	131.	B	171.	A
12.	E	52.	B	92.	C	132.	B	172.	C
13.	A	53.	A	93.	A	133.	D	173.	A
14.	B	54.	B	94.	E	134.	E	174.	A
15.	E	55.	B	95.	D	135.	A	175.	D
16.	D	56.	B	96.	D	136.	D	176.	C
17.	A	57.	A	97.	E	137.	B	177.	B
18.	E	58.	A	98.	C	138.	A	178.	C
19.	C	59.	A	99.	D	139.	D	179.	D
20.	B	60.	E	100.	E	140.	A	180.	D
21.	E	61.	A	101.	E	141.	D	181.	D
22.	A	62.	D	102.	A	142.	A	182.	D
23.	B	63.	A	103.	A	143.	C	183.	B
24.	C	64.	E	104.	A	144.	A	184.	D
25.	C	65.	C	105.	B	145.	B	185.	A
26.	C	66.	A	106.	C	146.	C	186.	C
27.	D	67.	D	107.	B	147.	A	187.	C
28.	A	68.	A	108.	C	148.	B	188.	D
29.	A	69.	E	109.	C	149.	C	189.	B
30.	A	70.	D	110.	E	150.	B	190.	C
31.	B	71.	C	111.	A	151.	E	191.	C
32.	B	72.	B	112.	C	152.	B	192.	B
33.	B	73.	B	113.	A	153.	B	193.	B
34.	C	74.	C	114.	C	154.	A	194.	D
35.	E	75.	C	115.	C	155.	E	195.	D
36.	D	76.	A	116.	C	156.	A	196.	E
37.	C	77.	E	117.	E	157.	E	197.	C
38.	C	78.	D	118.	C	158.	D	198.	D
39.	E	79.	D	119.	A	159.	C	199.	E
40.	D	80.	A	120.	D	160.	C	200.	A

EXPLANATORY ANSWERS
SAMPLE TEST 2

1. (B) The reality principle is served by the secondary process; it serves to distinguish reality from fantasy and is a function of the ego. The pleasure principle is a function of the id.

2. (A) Few psychologists have done research on taste; Pfaffman is the most famous contemporary experimenter in this area.

3. (E) Impulses travel from the pyramidal cells of the frontal cortex (which give rise to voluntary motor impulses), downward on the pyramidal tracts.

4. (A) In the motor area of the cortex, located in the pre-central gyrus of the cerebral hemisphere, are the large pyramidally-shaped cells which control voluntary movement.

5. (A) The nerve cells in lower animals are specialized for particular sensory-motor functions. During the course of evolution, as brains became larger, there developed an increasing number of cells without such particular functions. These are evident in the association area of the human cerebral cortex.

6. (E) A tropism is defined as an unlearned orienting movement of the whole organism which causes it to move toward or away from the stimulus. An example is a moth flying into a flame.

7. (A) The larger the magnitude of the stimulus, the larger it is perceived as being. Thus, the correlation is positive.

8. (C) The wave length of red is 700 millimicrons; orange is about 650 millimicrons, and blue is about 450 millimicrons.

9. (E) Rods deal with achromatic vision, while cones deal with color vision. This theory was discovered by von Kries.

10. (D) A test must discriminate between subjects at different levels of ability; it must yield the same scores on repeated measures; it must measure what it is purporting to measure.

11. (A) Several experimental studies have shown that on adult tests of intelligence, professional people score higher than skilled laborers, who score higher than unskilled workers.

12. (E) The variance is a measure of range and is equal to the square of the standard deviation.

13. (A) It has been found that a rat is more likely to surmount an obstacle for maternal motivation than for hunger motivation, and least of all for exploration motivation.

14. (B) Interoceptive stimulation is from the viscera; a neonate is not as sensitive to stimulation from the muscles or to external stimulation.

15. (E) Tolman's experiments in maze learning with rats attempt to show that learning is purposive (goal-oriented).

16. (D) Autistic thinking is loaded with fantasy elements; it is not connected

with reality; thus, autistic thinking and daydreaming are synonymous.

17. (A) Hull felt that learning required both habit strength and drive; his theory postulated that habits are hierarchial in the amount of strength that they possess.

18. (E) It has been empirically shown that a sharp clap can create strong, even traumatic fear in an infant.

19. (C) Wechsler is famous for his work on adult intelligence; he devised the Wechsler Adult Intelligence Scale, which is the most widely used instrument in the measurement of adult intelligence.

20. (B) Paranoia is a psychotic condition which is characterized by delusions of grandeur and/or of persecution. Paranoids generally express their symptoms very lucidly.

21. (E) Adler felt that man creates his own personality, and feelings of superiority and inferiority develop as the person develops; these feelings are not thought to be present at birth.

22. (A) Experimental work has shown that a shock reaction involves a decrease in pulse rate and an increase in the strength (amplitude) of the heartbeat.

23. (B) Anosmia is a condition in which smell is impaired.

24. (C) Overcompensation is a mechanism used when the person cannot cope with his real situation; the stress of overcompensation leads to the symptom of anxiety.

25. (C) Jung and Freud both believed that psychic energy was to be found in the libido. However, Jung did not believe that all libidinal energy was sexual in nature, as did Freud.

26. (C) The statement presented here is Thorndike's Law of Effect. His position was later changed to one where he deemphasized the latter half of the statement dealing with the role of punishment.

27. (D) Cattell was a pioneer psychometrician, who is known for devising many aptitudes and abilities tests, including what we now know as the College Entrance Examinations.

28. (A) Psychologists now believe that instinct plays only a minute part in human behavior; McDougall's work is no longer given very serious consideration, except from a historical point of view.

29. (A) Events in the past, traumatic enough to cause guilt and shame, can be remembered in treatment.

30. (A) An event may either occur or not occur. Sure occurrence is generally represented as 1.0 and sure non-occurrence is generally represented as 0, other possibilities being represented as having values between 1.0 and 0.

31. (B) Ebbinghaus is known for his work in retention and forgetting; he experimentally demonstrated the first forgetting curve, in which it is shown that forgetting occurs very rapidly at first and then drops off more slowly. He did most of his work with nonsense syllables.

32. (B) Spearman is an English psychologist who formulated the theory that in intelligence testing two factors exist: a general factor, common to all tests, and a specific factor, unique for each test.

33. (B) Gardner Murphy held that personality development was an interaction of biological and social forces; hence, he called his theory "Bio-social."

34. (C) In split-half reliability testing, scores on one half of the test are correlated with scores on the other half. A high correlation indicates high split-half reliability.

35. (E) In the most general sense, a threshold is the point where a response just barely occurs. In other words, the concept of threshold is synonymous with the concept of boundary, or lower limit.

36. (D) Frequency is not a measure of average, or central tendency, while the mean, median and mode all are measures of the average.

37. (C) The sociogram indicates choice preferences between different members of the group; it can be used to see which pupils would choose which other pupils in the group.

38. (C) The results of tests in the first grade are usually quite predictive; only tests given in the first few years of life are quite unlikely to correlate with later tests of intelligence or ability.

39. (E) Dewey was concerned with motivating the child from within; he did not believe that any external pressures or motivations are moral or meaningful ways to motivate the child.

40. (D) Because the shy pupil is not an overt behavior problem, and just because his difficulty does not manifest itself in a conspicuous way, he is more likely to be overlooked than children who present more overt behavior problems.

41. (C) Knowledge of the alphabet is not conclusive proof of reading readiness, while clear and spontaneous speech, adequate vision and coordination, and satisfactory performance on a reading readiness test offer more conclusive evidence of reading readiness.

42. (B) Reading from left to right does not occur naturally; it is the correct direction in our culture but not in other cultures, and it must be taught.

43. (A) The objective of determinative epidemiologic research is to discover relations between the way of life or the environment of a population and the prevalence or severity of the disease. For this reason considerable use is made of correlation analysis in epidemiology.

44. (D) It is rare that children from the first to third grades will select their friends because of sex. Girls and boys play with one another quite readily at the early ages.

45. (B) It may be necessary for the teacher to understand motives of the behavior of a child who is presenting particularly puzzling problems in the classroom situation.

46. (E) Kilpatrick has been one of the modern leaders of progressive education; another leader in progressive education was John Dewey.

47. (D) Culture-fair tests were designed just because most verbal-oriented intelligence tests tend to discriminate against those in lower socio-economic classes. Culture-fair tests are designed to remove this bias by eliminating the effects of different backgrounds.

48. (C) Before a recent court decision, parents were not allowed to know their child's IQ scores; now, they can know the score if they request the information from the school.

49. (A) The bulletin board is a traditional feature in all classrooms, and is not related to reading readiness programs.

50. (D) Hutchins is noted as a progressive educator; he was president of the University of Chicago. He has not done work in intelligence testing.

51. (E) The Wechsler scales, for both children and adults, involve both verbal and performance measures of intelligence. The scales had offered the promise of being a diagnostic instrument for certain personality disturbances, but this promise has hardly been fulfilled.

52. (B) A trace conditioned response reverses traditional time relationships in conditioning and is the most difficult form of conditioning to establish.

53. (A) Klüver and Lashley have done extensive work in discrimination; Lashley is particularly known for a piece of apparatus, used in discrimination learning experiments, called the Lashley jumping stand.

54. (B) In 1942 Sheldon's research demonstrated that viscerotonia (love of

comfort, people and food) correlates highest with endomorphy. Cerebrotonia (restraint and over-all inhibition) correlates highly with ectomorphy; while the active, adventurous somatotone correlates highly with mesomorphy.

55. (B) Very intense stimuli will fire a neuron even in the relative refractory phase. Thus, more firings can occur in a shorter period of time. This refers to the concept of temporal summation - an additive effect of more neuron firings under bombardment from strong stimuli.

56. (B) Lower IQs are generally found among deaf rather than blind children; this indicates the auditory modality may be more important than the visual one in influencing intelligence development.

57. (A) Most mentally defective persons do not have a clearly defined biological defect such as mongolism, etc.; they are classified in the category of undifferentiated amentia.

58. (A) Since IQ equals MA divided by CA, the child's IQ at age 4 is 80. If his IQ is constant, it will be 80 at age 10.

59. (A) Schizophrenia may have organic bases. The other mental disorders are always classified as functional psychoses: they are disorders of psychological origin without clearly defined tangible cause or structural change.

60. (E) Aphasia is the impairment or loss of ability to articulate words or comprehend speech. Henry Head distinguished four classes: verbal defect, syntactical defect, nominal defect and semantic defect.

61. (A) The WISC is standardized so that it yields a lower score (for the same relative performance) than the 1937 Stanford Binet Scale.

62. (D) The Wechsler Scale is the only test of intelligence which includes a subscale of factual information.

63. (A) Terman and Merrill have shown that superior children show greater fluctuating changes in IQ than average children. The IQs of the average children tend to remain rather constant over time.

64. (E) Extinction will occur when the conditioned stimulus is repeatedly presented without some sort of reinforcement.

65. (C) The individual described here is not repressing his unpleasant thoughts; rather, he is isolating or compartmentalizing them.

66. (A) A difference as great as or greater than the one observed could be expected to occur purely by chance. No more often than one time in a hundred means that an observed difference is significant at the one percent level.

67. (D) Fugue applies to neurotic behavior involving some episode, which the individual, when he recovers, is unable to recall. Hence, he has repressed the episode.

68. (A) Rank is known for his psychoanalytically based theory of "birth-trauma."

69. (E) Guthrie is a learning theorist connected with a theory of one-trial learning. Tolman is the learning theorist connected with Sign Learning.

70. (D) Repression is a defense mechanism in which an impulse or memory which might provoke feelings of guilt is denied by its disappearance from awareness.

71. (C) According to Freud, the psychosexual stages of development are the following: oral, anal, phallic, latency and genital.

72. (B) An hysterical disturbance is one in which anxiety is "converted" into some bodily malfunction when there is nothing organically wrong with the body. Psychoanalytic treatment of hysteria is most frequently unsuccessful.

73. (B) Sullivan's social-oriented theory of personality development holds that close "chum" friendships most characteristically develop in the pre-adolescent period.

74. (C) Fromm-Reichman is associated with the general area of therapy, but not with child therapy, while the others mentioned are specifically known for their research in child therapy.

75. (C) Piaget refers to speech which is centered in the ego so that the child cannot listen from the standpoint of the person he is talking to; in other words, ego-centric speech precludes empathic speech.

76. (A) While the Wecshler scales had been thought to be a promising instrument in diagnoses, empirical evidence has cast doubt on this promise, although it has not been completely eliminated.

77. (E) Arithmetic and Digit Span tests on the Wechsler are the scales which most require good concentration for successful performance.

78. (D) Change in average IQ does not mean that individual IQs have changed; rather, in high school, the brighter students are likely still to be in school, so that higher IQ on the average is the result of a different average population.

79. (D) Aptitude tests measure a person's specific abilities at various types of activities, while intelligence tests tap more general cognitive functioning. The two types of measures do not usually show a high correlation.

80. (A) The median is not as affected by extreme scores as is the mean; hence, it is better to use the median in a distribution with extreme scores.

81. (A) Content validity refers literally to the seeming, or face validity of the test based on the item content. It is not like criterion validity in that it attempts to measure correlations between two measures.

82. (C) 68 percent of all observations fall between ± 1 sigma by definition and:

95.5 percent fall between ± 2 sigma
99.7 percent fall between ± 3 sigma
99.99 percent fall between ± 4 sigma

83. (A) The reliability of a test indicates how consistent a measure it is; if a person does very well on a reliable measure of intelligence compared to his group, he should place high on another intelligence test (measuring the same thing) if both tests are reliable measures.

84. (B) In vocational abilities testing, validity is usually predictive validity. The criterion is thus particularly important; the test should correlate well with the best measure of job success.

85. (A) Gestalt psychologists are particularly involved with the study of perceptual phenomena. They feel the most important aspects of perception are based on perceptual configurations, and not on isolated aspects of the perceptual field.

86. (E) Behavioristic theorists describe all aspects of the functioning organism in terms of his overt behaviors, or habits.

87. (C) Observations recorded on the control group are used as estimates of what the experimental group observations would have been had the members of the group not been exposed to the test conditions.

88. (E) Experimental research in perception of personality has shown that judgments usually are based on first impressions; more information adds confidence, but does not increase accuracy of judgment.

89. (B) Work on the relationship between intelligence and creativity has been done by Barron. He has found that, for subjects of high ability, those who score high on tests of intelligence may not score high on tests of creativity, and vice versa.

90. (C) The object of an instinct is anything which can satisfy the aim of the instinct. All instincts have the aim of reducing the organism to a state of quiescence.

91. (C) Before the ego develops, and perceptions based on ego processes take place, energy is less bound, and more freely displaceable.

92. (C) Fromm feels that the true concept of love is impossible in a world where love objects are valued for their "market" worth; that is, in terms of a commodity, not in terms of the satisfaction of personal needs or goals.

93. (A) Fromm feels that much of the dilemma of modern man is living without the previous restrictions, but without a fully developed self. Although man is free, he does not know what to do with his freedom, and tries to escape from it.

94. (E) Twenty-five percent of the scores fall between the 50th percentile (the median) and the 75th percentile (the third quartile).

95. (D) Neurosis can be treated more easily in humans than in laboratory animals. Parenthetically, it has been shown that neurotic animals may resort to alcohol if they are given the opportunity.

96. (D) Guthrie believes in a one-trial learning theory; he therefore does not place emphasis on practice, since he feels learning is an all or none thing.

97. (E) Readiness is usually a concept in educational psychology; it is not a principle of perception as formulated by the Gestalt theorists.

98. (C) For example, the "median" may be better than the "mean" as an indicator of the income of a typical dentist when a few of the dentists have either an unusually high or an unusually low income.

99. (D) Maslow assumes a tremendous constancy in human needs, so that the relative strength of needs is constant in the individual throughout his life.

100. (E) The concept of animism refers to the attribution of life or life-like qualities to inanimate objects. It is usually found in very young children.

101. (E) Reaction formation is a defense mechanism in which a subject denies a disapproved motive through giving strong expression to its opposite.

102. (A) Frequently, the paranoid who claims that he is being persecuted actually has the desire to punish or persecute his supposed assailants; he is thus projecting.

103. (A) Rejecting a true hypothesis is known as an alpha error or Type I error. Accepting a false hypothesis is known as a beta error or Type II error.

104. (A) One of the chief common characteristics of all behavior disorders is the display of violently intense emotional reactions.

105. (B) According to Freudian theory, repression of a memory will occur when it will arouse too much anxiety to allow the individual to function normally.

106. (C) The basic requirement for the occurrence of any of the defense mechanisms is an internal thought or tendency judged to be unacceptable; this tendency cannot be dealt with realistically, and so it is distorted to be acceptable by a defense mechanism.

107. (B) Isolation refers to a compartmentalization - that is, a separation in memory - of unacceptable thoughts and recollections. It is not a part of the obsessive-compulsive neurosis.

108. (C) Repression inhibits fear from generalizing appropriately. What the individual is really bothered by is repressed; the fear of some object is the surface manifestation of the phobia.

109. (C) Sociograms just indicate choices and rejections; they show the pattern of choice, but do not give any information as to why this pattern exists.

110. (E) Reaction formation is a defense mechanism in which a subject denies a disapproved motive by giving strong expression to its opposite.

111. (A) Binet first proposed the concept of the intelligence quotient about the turn of the century.

112. (C) The Guess Who technique is designed to measure social choices and relationships in the classroom; since it describes a pattern of social choices, it is a sociometric technique.

113. (A) Psychometric instruments for infants are not valid for predicting future status; they can be used to see how the child stands in developmental terms; that is, they can be used in a purely normative sense.

114. (C) Most psychometric measures used today are structured (with the exception, of course, of the projective tests). A great number of tests have been devised to measure cognitive abilities in general, and these are widely used today.

115. (C) The minimum requirement for a diagnostic instrument is that it discriminate between normal and abnormal subjects. Wechsler's scales have not met with significant success in making such a differentiation.

116. (C) Repression is a defense mechanism in which an impulse or memory which might provoke feelings of guilt is denied by its disappearance from awareness.

117. (E) The phenomenon described here is the phenomenon of insight. Koffka is a Gestalt psychologist and the Gestaltists were the first school to elaborate on the phenomenon of insight.

118. (C) A percentile ranking is a measure to place a person relative to the rest of the group. The percentile one achieves indicates what percent of the group he did better than.

119. (A) It is usual that those with high intelligence scores will do well in school and score well on tests of achievement. The correlation is positive, except in the case of underachievers, who score well on intelligence tests, but not on achievement tests.

120. (D) Systematic sampling is one of a number of sampling techniques used to help ensure that a sample is appropriately representative of the population. A random method is often used in selecting the first member of the sample.

121. (A) Split-half coefficients usually yield higher reliabilities than test-retest coefficients, since the latter are lowered by factors intervening over the time period. The split-half technique uses data obtained in one sitting by the same subject.

122. (B) When we correlate a test and a criterion measure, we are examining the validity of the test, rather than the reliability. We are asking how well the test correlates with the criterion variable, or how well it predicts behavior.

123. (A) Reliability measures the ordering of the same subjects when the same or equivalent test is given at some future time. The higher the reliability, the more likely is the ordering of the test to be similar.

124. (D) The Kuder-Richardson formula is a correction formula for the split-half method of determining reliability. Another formula used for correcting a split-half coefficient is the Spearman-Brown formula.

125. (D) The Q technique was developed by Stephenson for the study of self-perception. The subject sorts statements from those least applicable to himself to those most applicable to himself; at the outset, the middle piles will be largest, and the sort will have a normal shape. The large middle piles will contain statements of ambiguous applicability.

126. (A) Variations among repeated measurements of the same physical quantity commonly display a surprising degree of regularity. A distribution of

such measurements is known as a normal distribution. The graph of a normal distribution forms a bell-shaped curve that extends indefinitely in both directions, coming closer and closer to the horizontal axis without ever reaching it. An important feature of any normal distribution is that it is symmetrical about its mean.

127. (B) The Hawthorne effect was found in a famous experiment in social-industrial psychology. Workers who were "watched" by the experimenters performed better, no matter what their treatment condition was. The knowledge that they were under observation seemed to be the important variable.

128. (D) Allport is a cognitively-oriented personality theorist who feels that traits are the most stable aspects of personality, and the attitudes and intentions must also be studied to get at a complete picture of the personality.

129. (C)

$$\left[\frac{1}{N-1}\Sigma n(X - X_{avg})^2\right]^{1/2}$$

130. (E)

n	X	X_{avg}	$X - X_{avg}$
3	2.1	2.5	-0.4
7	2.2		-0.3
11	2.3		-0.2
18	2.4		-0.1
22	2.5		0.0
16	2.6		0.1
11	2.7		0.2
7	2.8		0.3
3	2.9		0.4
2	3.0		0.5

$(X - X_{avg})^2$	$n(X - X_{avg})^2$
0.16	0.48
0.09	0.63
0.04	0.44
0.01	0.18
0.00	0.00
0.01	0.16
0.04	0.44
0.09	0.63
0.16	0.48
0.25	0.50
	$3.94 = \Sigma n(X - X_{avg})^2$

$$S^2 = \frac{1}{n-1}\Sigma n(X - X_{avg})^2$$

$$= \frac{1}{99} \times 3.94 = 0.0398$$

S = 0.20 approximately

131. (B) This curve represents a normal distribution.

132. (B) This curve represents a normal distribution.

133. (D) This is the typical negatively accelerated learning curve.

134. (E) An ogive is a S-shaped curve.

135. (A) Note that the high scores are lumped together; no discrimination is made among them.

136. (D) Higher organisms have what is called a synaptic nervous system, where impulses are conducted along specific pathways. Each neuron has a nucleus, or cell body; it has dendrites, which carry impulses toward the cell body, and axons, which carry impulses away from the cell body. There is no plasma in the neuron.

137. (B) The efferent neuron leaves the cell body and will activate some muscle effector. The afferent neuron, on the other hand, originates in receptors and has sensory functions.

138. (A) The period after an impulse has passed and the nerve fiber has undergone depolarization is called the absolute refractory period. During this time, no stimulation, no matter how intense, can start a nerve impulse.

139. (D) There is a designated receptive area for each of these senses in the cortex; thus, messages from visual receptors end up in a visual area, and messages from auditory receptors end up in an auditory area of the cortex.

140. (A) In order for a message to get from one neuron to another, it must bridge a gap called a synapse. Thus, unless an impulse passes across a synapse, its communication stops.

141. (D) If overt behavior is the only legitimate subject matter for psychology, it follows that the non-overt states of conscious experience cannot be studied scientifically.

142. (A) Any insights that we can obtain into the behavior of any organism will contribute to psychology. Hence, animal behavior is a legitimate subject for study in and of itself.

143. (C) An operant is a response in the behavioral repertory of the animal which he can make freely without any reinforcement; reinforcement will strengthen an operant and increase the probability of its occurrence.

144. (A) A fixed ratio schedule refers to reinforcement of the animal after a fixed number of operant responses; a fixed interval schedule refers to reinforcing the animal after a fixed time period, no matter what response he has made.

145. (B) Instrumental conditioning gets its name because the subject's actions are instrumental in bringing about this reward. Thus, when the subject makes the correct response, reinforcement occurs.

146. (C) The animal will respond very rapidly, unless many responses are required between reinforcements.

147. (A) Skinner and his followers are responsible for the experimentation done in operant conditioning and in developing different schedules of conditioning.

148. (B) Any stimulus that is associated with a primary reinforcer (say, food) is called a secondary reinforcer; it comes to acquire reward properties of its own.

149. (C) When we are reinforced periodically and never know when the reinforcement will come, we are on a variable ratio schedule. This situation is similar to gambling.

150. (B) Analysis of variance is a technique for testing whether a set of two or more sample means can be taken to be random samples from the same population. The term F is the ratio of the variances of the sets of data.

151. (E) Schachter and Singer have shown that emotion is a joint function of cognition and state of physiological arousal; both are necessary for emotion to occur. Different emotions arise from the same state of physiological arousal; the nature of these emotions depends on the available cognitions.

152. (B) The James-Lange theory holds that the emotion is merely our perception of the visceral change; Schachter's theory holds that visceral change is necessary for emotional functioning to occur, but cognitions are also needed.

153. (B) Cannon refuted the James-Lange theory but did not state the nature of visceral changes between emotions.

154. (A) Since the subject would have totally inappropriate cognitions, he would be even more susceptible to "contaging" the emotion from his angry companion; we would expect more emotional behavior from him.

155. (E) Since emotion is a joint function of cognition and physiological arousal, these subjects can show emotion only if they have arousal. They would not have arousal with a placebo injection, unless they were self-aroused.

156. (A) Regression analysis is a procedure for the fitting of a line or curve to a set of data and the using of the line or curve for the estimating of a dependent variable or function.

157. (E) Field theory is a molar approach; it takes configuration rather than detail into account; relationships and configurations are more important to perception than individual details in the perceptual field.

158. (D) In order to reduce tension, it is necessary that the person come into contact with the satisfying goal region, or some equivalent. The locomotion can be real, substitute, or vicarious in nature.

159. (C) Lewin attempted to develop a psychology based on topological mathematics, using hodological space, which is non-Euclidean.

160. (C) With maturity, Lewin holds that there is greater differentiation between the boundaries of different regions.

161. (B) The design and procedural format of a clinical trial are determined largely by the type of data and method of management of data decided upon to test the hypothesis upon which the trial is based.

162. (D) Guthrie, a learning theorist, holds that learning is one trial, and what we learn are movements, not acts.

163. (E) According to Guthrie, movement-produced stimuli are what are relevant in learning. These stimuli occur within the subject, and at this time, we cannot measure them, since we do not have the methods. However, the model assumes that the cue and response must occur at the same point in time for learning to occur.

164. (D) Learning occurs when the movement-produced stimuli become conditioned to the movement; this happens in one trial. Guthrie feels that complex acts may not appear to be learned in a one-trial way, but each separate component of the act is learned in one trial.

165. (D) The movements are the important dependent variable, not the skills or the complex acts which grow out of the separate movements.

166. (A) In a one-trial learning theory, we would predict that when the organism is again presented with the same combination of stimuli, the exact response (series of movements) will occur.

167. (E) Cerebellum refers to that portion of the brain which controls balance and coordinated motor activity. The limbic activity of survival, identified by Broca, MacLean and Pribram, includes: thalamus and hypothalamus, amygdala, hippocampus, septum and cingulate gyrus.

168. (B) Dissonance theory is a social psychological theory which accounts for post-decisional behaviors. Resonance theory, frequency theory, volleyplace theory and Von Beksy's theory are all theoretical explanations of auditory phenomena.

169. (A) Stimulus-response theories prefer to find observable intermediaries such as movements which can explain behavior. Some learning theorists such as Hull do use non-observable intermediaries, such as conditioned inhibition; these must be inferred from behavior.

170. (A) Guthrie is a stimulus response theorist and Tolman is a cognitive theorist; both believe that contiguity of stimulus and response in time and space, and not reinforcement, are necessary for learning to occur.

171. (A) An intervening variable exists purely for the sake of aiding some theoretical explanation; it has no measurable meaning in itself. A hypothetical construct is another type of intermediary variable which does, hypothetically, exist, although we cannot measure it at the present time with the present state of knowledge.

172. (C) When we want to correlate the rank orders of two bodies of data (say, rank in the class on math tests and on English tests), we use the Spearman rho. For non-ranked data, the Pearson product moment correlation technique is used.

173. (A) A tract is a bundle of nerves in the CNS which has the same points of origin and termination, and the same function. But the nerves of a fasciculus may have different functions, although they have the same points of origin and termination. Both tracts and fasciculi travel in close proximity to each other up and down the spinal cord, but neither can be found in the peripheral nervous system, since by definition, a tract can only be in the CNS.

174. (A) This type of theorizing is behavioral in nature; behavioral therapy is concerned with redirecting overt

behavior. For example, in treating a phobia, the behavioral therapist is concerned with ridding the person of the specific phobia, and not with treating the underlying symptoms.

175. (D) Skinner is a behavioral psychologist who has worked extensively with instrumental conditioning; recent projects of his have involved attempts at conditioning therapy on schizophrenics.

176. (C) According to behaviorist therapy, underlying symptoms are not relevant to treatment; the therapist should concentrate only on the overt symptom.

177. (B) Shaping up is a behaviorist concept; it refers to teaching the correct response by giving reinforcements as the organism gets nearer to the response (to show him what the "right track" is).

178. (C) The subject is rewarded for making the correct response in the hope that he will learn this response and that other non-reinforced responses will be extinguished.

179. (D) The thalamus takes raw sensations and adds not only amplification, but a quality or hedonic tone. This is a mood tone which gives an affective or emotional quality to these raw sensations. If the fibers of the thalamus are cut, physical pain cannot be easily induced, but what pain is felt is usually severe and intractable; that is, the pain is central - experienced directly in the thalamus - and not transmitted from the peripheral senses.

180. (D) In a normal distribution, 95.45 percent of the observations fall between two standard deviations above the mean and two standard deviations below the mean.

181. (D) Classical conditioning merely involves the repeated pairing of some conditioned stimulus with the unconditioned stimulus; after a time, the conditioned stimulus, when presented alone, will elicit a conditioned response which is very similar to the unconditioned response originally elicited by the unconditioned stimulus.

182. (D) The conditioned response is essentially the same as the unconditioned response; it is elicited by the unconditioned stimulus before and after conditioning, and the conditioned stimulus after conditioning.

183. (B) Skinner believes that there are two kinds of conditioning; respondent (classical) and operant (instrumental). Respondent conditioning involves involuntary smooth muscle, and operant conditioning involves voluntary, or striated muscle.

184. (D) Usually, the conditioned stimulus is presented about one-half second before the unconditioned stimulus. In backward conditioning, the reverse occurs: the unconditioned stimulus is presented before the conditioned stimulus. This process does not always produce conditioning.

185. (A) A person can move from one region to another in Lewin's system. Such changes of interest in the various life-space regions are called locomotion. Communication refers to the mutual influence regions of the person have on one another. Innerpersonal cells may communicate with one another; the perceptual region communicates with the inner-personal region, and so on.

186. (C) Structuralism, which began with Wundt's research, was interested in analyzing the conscious experience in terms of its structural makeup (that is, in terms of sensations and images).

187. (C) Functionalists emphasized the functions rather than the contents of consciousness. They had a psychology of adjustment; they were not interested in learning what the basic components of consciousness were, but rather in discovering the functions of these components in adjustment.

188. (D) Structuralists were not interested in overt phenomena; therefore, they did not study reflexes, which played

no part in the structure of conscious experience.

189. (B) In structuralist language, the observer is the person who introspects; today we refer to the observer as some objective psychologist who is watching the subject under different controlled experimental conditions.

190. (C) Prevalence of decayed, missing, and filled teeth (DMFT) among children and young adults is also an approximation of total experience with dental caries since DMF teeth at those ages are nearly all the result of dental caries.

191. (C) Non-parametric tests are less rigid in their assumption about the data; therefore, when the variable does not meet assumptions such as normally required by parametric tests, we use non-parametric measures.

192. (B) Analysis of variance is a parametric statistic requiring normally distributed interval data.

193. (B) We are likely to use non-parametric tests on ordinal or ratio data where no mean can be obtained. With ordinal data, we can legitimately compute the median.

194. (D) The rank-sum test is used to test the difference between two medians. If we had parametric data, we could use a t-test to test the difference between two means.

195. (D) We can use the parametric technique of product-moment correlation to determine the linear relationship between two variables if these variables are both continuous and normally distributed; otherwise, it is necessary to use non-parametric methods.

196. (E) Interval and ratio data are based on scales where the units are equal; ordinal and ratio scales do not have equal units.

197. (C) In the Muller-Lyer illusion, figure B appears larger than figure A, but they are actually the same length.

198. (D) Illusions are false perceptions; what we perceive is different from what is objectively measured. In the Muller-Lyer illusion, size constancy is belied, and we see the lines as being of different size, when they are the same size.

199. (E) The constancies and organizational effects (relationships between figure and ground) create a disparity between proximal stimulation and appearance.

200. (A) The phi-phenomenon is commonly produced by turning on and off two separated stationary sources. As the first is turned off and the second is turned on, we perceive a spot of light moving from the first source to the second.

GRE ADVANCED TEST IN PSYCHOLOGY

SAMPLE TEST 3

Time: 2 hours and 50 minutes

Directions: Select from the lettered choices that choice which best completes the statement or answers the question. Write the letter of your choice on the answer sheet.

1. Obtaining a goal leads to

   A. increase in the need related to the goal
   B. operant conditioning
   C. instrumental learning
   D. intensification of drives related to the goal-object
   E. reduction of the drive state

2. The term "absolute threshold" refers to

   A. the behavioral distinction between man and animals
   B. the difference between the upper and lower limits of perception
   C. the greatest stimulus intensity which can be endured without pain
   D. the least amount of energy which can be registered by a sense organ
   E. the upper limit of perception

3. "Avoidance learning"

   A. is a term coined by William James
   B. can be used to explain the rapidity with which extinction sometimes occurs
   C. is illustrated by the rat which learns that shock will not be delivered if it presses a lever
   D. is illustrated by the rat which learns that shock can be turned off by pressing a lever
   E. is synonymous with escape learning

4. The ethnocentric personality is a description often applied to individuals who

   A. best express the typical personality of their culture
   B. believe that all cultural groups are inferior to their own
   C. are sociometrically popular in their subgroup
   D. belong to minority groups with great status in the society
   E. belong to any minority groups in the society

5. The three dimensions of meaning which are usually obtained with the Semantic Differential are

   A. evaluative, activity, potency
   B. schizoid, cycloid, eurythmic
   C. extroversion-introversion, surgency-desurgency, integration-differentiation
   D. value, importance, veracity
   E. aesthetic, social, religious

6. In classical conditioning studies, the "unconditioned stimulus"

   A. elicits a response before any training has taken place
   B. becomes the conditioned stimulus
   C. becomes the conditioned response
   D. ceases to elicit an automatic response
   E. produces an operant response

ANSWER SHEET TEST (3)

No.					
1	A	B	C	D	E
2	A	B	C	D	E
3	A	B	C	D	E
4	A	B	C	D	E
5	A	B	C	D	E
6	A	B	C	D	E
7	A	B	C	D	E
8	A	B	C	D	E
9	A	B	C	D	E
10	A	B	C	D	E
11	A	B	C	D	E
12	A	B	C	D	E
13	A	B	C	D	E
14	A	B	C	D	E
15	A	B	C	D	E
16	A	B	C	D	E
17	A	B	C	D	E
18	A	B	C	D	E
19	A	B	C	D	E
20	A	B	C	D	E
21	A	B	C	D	E
22	A	B	C	D	E
23	A	B	C	D	E
24	A	B	C	D	E
25	A	B	C	D	E
26	A	B	C	D	E
27	A	B	C	D	E
28	A	B	C	D	E
29	A	B	C	D	E
30	A	B	C	D	E
31	A	B	C	D	E
32	A	B	C	D	E
33	A	B	C	D	E
34	A	B	C	D	E
35	A	B	C	D	E
36	A	B	C	D	E
37	A	B	C	D	E
38	A	B	C	D	E
39	A	B	C	D	E
40	A	B	C	D	E
41	A	B	C	D	E
42	A	B	C	D	E
43	A	B	C	D	E
44	A	B	C	D	E
45	A	B	C	D	E
46	A	B	C	D	E
47	A	B	C	D	E
48	A	B	C	D	E
49	A	B	C	D	E
50	A	B	C	D	E
51	A	B	C	D	E
52	A	B	C	D	E
53	A	B	C	D	E
54	A	B	C	D	E
55	A	B	C	D	E
56	A	B	C	D	E
57	A	B	C	D	E
58	A	B	C	D	E
59	A	B	C	D	E
60	A	B	C	D	E
61	A	B	C	D	E
62	A	B	C	D	E
63	A	B	C	D	E
64	A	B	C	D	E
65	A	B	C	D	E
66	A	B	C	D	E
67	A	B	C	D	E
68	A	B	C	D	E
69	A	B	C	D	E
70	A	B	C	D	E
71	A	B	C	D	E
72	A	B	C	D	E
73	A	B	C	D	E
74	A	B	C	D	E
75	A	B	C	D	E
76	A	B	C	D	E
77	A	B	C	D	E
78	A	B	C	D	E
79	A	B	C	D	E
80	A	B	C	D	E
81	A	B	C	D	E
82	A	B	C	D	E
83	A	B	C	D	E
84	A	B	C	D	E
85	A	B	C	D	E
86	A	B	C	D	E
87	A	B	C	D	E
88	A	B	C	D	E
89	A	B	C	D	E
90	A	B	C	D	E
91	A	B	C	D	E
92	A	B	C	D	E
93	A	B	C	D	E
94	A	B	C	D	E
95	A	B	C	D	E
96	A	B	C	D	E
97	A	B	C	D	E
98	A	B	C	D	E
99	A	B	C	D	E
100	A	B	C	D	E
101	A	B	C	D	E
102	A	B	C	D	E
103	A	B	C	D	E
104	A	B	C	D	E
105	A	B	C	D	E
106	A	B	C	D	E
107	A	B	C	D	E
108	A	B	C	D	E
109	A	B	C	D	E
110	A	B	C	D	E
111	A	B	C	D	E
112	A	B	C	D	E
113	A	B	C	D	E
114	A	B	C	D	E
115	A	B	C	D	E
116	A	B	C	D	E
117	A	B	C	D	E
118	A	B	C	D	E
119	A	B	C	D	E
120	A	B	C	D	E
121	A	B	C	D	E
122	A	B	C	D	E
123	A	B	C	D	E
124	A	B	C	D	E
125	A	B	C	D	E
126	A	B	C	D	E
127	A	B	C	D	E
128	A	B	C	D	E
129	A	B	C	D	E
130	A	B	C	D	E
131	A	B	C	D	E
132	A	B	C	D	E
133	A	B	C	D	E
134	A	B	C	D	E
135	A	B	C	D	E
136	A	B	C	D	E
137	A	B	C	D	E
138	A	B	C	D	E
139	A	B	C	D	E
140	A	B	C	D	E
141	A	B	C	D	E
142	A	B	C	D	E
143	A	B	C	D	E
144	A	B	C	D	E
145	A	B	C	D	E
146	A	B	C	D	E
147	A	B	C	D	E
148	A	B	C	D	E
149	A	B	C	D	E
150	A	B	C	D	E
151	A	B	C	D	E
152	A	B	C	D	E
153	A	B	C	D	E
154	A	B	C	D	E
155	A	B	C	D	E
156	A	B	C	D	E
157	A	B	C	D	E
158	A	B	C	D	E
159	A	B	C	D	E
160	A	B	C	D	E
161	A	B	C	D	E
162	A	B	C	D	E
163	A	B	C	D	E
164	A	B	C	D	E
165	A	B	C	D	E
166	A	B	C	D	E
167	A	B	C	D	E
168	A	B	C	D	E
169	A	B	C	D	E
170	A	B	C	D	E
171	A	B	C	D	E
172	A	B	C	D	E
173	A	B	C	D	E
174	A	B	C	D	E
175	A	B	C	D	E
176	A	B	C	D	E
177	A	B	C	D	E
178	A	B	C	D	E
179	A	B	C	D	E
180	A	B	C	D	E
181	A	B	C	D	E
182	A	B	C	D	E
183	A	B	C	D	E
184	A	B	C	D	E
185	A	B	C	D	E
186	A	B	C	D	E
187	A	B	C	D	E
188	A	B	C	D	E
189	A	B	C	D	E
190	A	B	C	D	E
191	A	B	C	D	E
192	A	B	C	D	E
193	A	B	C	D	E
194	A	B	C	D	E
195	A	B	C	D	E
196	A	B	C	D	E
197	A	B	C	D	E
198	A	B	C	D	E
199	A	B	C	D	E
200	A	B	C	D	E

7. Which of the following is not a measure of the variability of a set of scores?

   A. average deviation
   B. standard deviation
   C. variance
   D. deviation ratio
   E. square root of variance

8. Which of the following is the least accepted of Freud's notions today?

   A. the theory of infantile sexuality
   B. the notion that dreams have a psychodynamic meaning
   C. the notion that people can repress ideas out of consciousness
   D. the notion that humans have a death instinct
   E. the concept of reaction formation

9. The Luchins Water Jar test would most likely be employed in an experiment on

   A. autism
   B. perceptual defense
   C. sensory deprivation
   D. stimulus generalization
   E. set

10. The best definition of a reinforcement is that it is something

   A. which an organism likes
   B. which an organism either likes or dislikes
   C. which serves as a goal for the organism
   D. which motivates learning
   E. which reduces a drive state

11. "Drive-reduction" theory holds that the crucial factor determining what is learned is

   A. punishment
   B. frustration of drives
   C. contiguity of drive and stimulus
   D. reinforcement
   E. alleviation of needs

12. The object or condition which satisfies a motive is called a

   A. goal
   B. consummatory response
   C. valence
   D. fundamental reducer
   E. instrumental response

13. In Harlow's experiment on the affectional drives, baby monkeys were placed in an open field situation designed to evoke both fear and exploratory behavior. The monkeys were less fearful and more willing to explore when

   A. the milk-giving wire "mother" was present
   B. the cloth-covered "mother" was present
   C. neither "mother" was present
   D. the experimenter removed the strange objects
   E. either "mother" was present

14. In terms of Hullian reinforcement theory, money represents a

   A. secondary goal
   B. primary drive
   C. status drive
   D. primary reinforcement
   E. positive valence

15. Deprivation of a drive causes it to

   A. diminish
   B. dominate behavior
   C. gradually disappear
   D. change into some other drive
   E. immediately disappear

16. The term "non-directive" is best applied to

   A. skinnerian therapy
   B. narcoanalysis
   C. psychoanalysis
   D. client-centered therapy
   E. jungian therapy

17. Freud's final position regarding the defense mechanisms was that

   A. repression is the chief defense and is a basic component of all the other defenses
   B. they are used only by psychotics and severe neurotics

C. regression is the only activity which can genuinely be called a defense mechanism
D. each of them represents primarily an effort by the neurotic to control aggresive impulses
E. none of the above

18. If a person's level of aspiration is usually much higher than his performance level, he experiences

A. status enhancement
B. achievement
C. success
D. reinforcement
E. failure

19. If errors or mistakes are used as the measure of learning, the curve on a graph would

A. decrease from left to right
B. decrease from right to left
C. be flat from left to right
D. increase from left to right
E. increase from right to left

20. Increased response after a rest period in a series of extinction trials is termed

A. response regeneration
B. positive transfer
C. recuperation effect
D. spontaneous recovery
E. conditioned disinhibition

21. A plateau in a learning curve indicates

A. exhaustion
B. learning is complete
C. successful reinforcement
D. increased drive
E. a period of little or no improvement

22. Essay examinations, as a means of measuring retention, represent a form of

A. recognition method
B. savings method
C. memory-bank method
D. recall method
E. rote method

23. Learning <u>not to respond</u> to stimuli takes place in

A. habituation
B. extinction
C. desensitization
D. all of these
E. none of these

24. The learning of a sequence of responses, in which stimuli for one response arise from the previous response is called

A. serial learning
B. discrimination training
C. chaining
D. alternation learning
E. stimulus generalization

25. If a patient in psychoanalysis begins to feel angry and hostile towards his analyst, this would indicate

A. positive transference
B. negative transference
C. counter-transference
D. resistive functioning
E. induced transference

26. The best definition of anxiety is that it is

A. frustration produced by the environment
B. fear of an object
C. general uneasiness
D. the discomfort from repressing hostile impulses
E. fear of bodily harm

27. The best way to reduce a generalized fear is to

A. sublimate the drive
B. repress the anxiety
C. learn to discriminate between different situations
D. suppress the anxiety
E. do none of these

28. The approach gradient is

A. steeper than the avoidance gradient
B. a negative valence

C. stronger than the avoidance gradient near a goal
D. a positive valence
E. stronger than the avoidance gradient far from the goal

29. The Young-Helmholtz theory of color vision

A. asserts that brightness perception is dependent upon wavelength alone
B. denies the existence of primary colors
C. doesn't explain how color-blind persons can see white
D. holds that cones are sensitive to specific wavelengths
E. explains how color-blind persons can see white

30. A person who believes that smoking is beneficial because it reduces weight is probably

A. projecting
B. fixating
C. compensating
D. hallucinating
E. rationalizing

31. Allport's concept of functional autonomy and the notion of secondary drive are both

A. attempts to translate Freud's death instinct into more modern terms
B. attempts to explain the fact that children become more independent of their parents as they grow older
C. attempts to explain the existence of behavior which is not in the direct service of physiological drives
D. attempts to explain learning on a purely cognitive basis
E. derived from Jung

32. The "photochemical event" in vision is

A. the focusing action of the lens
B. the emission of retinene by the choroid layer
C. the decomposition and resynthesis of certain substances
D. the firing of the bipolar receptor cells
E. the action of the cones

33. The best way to see a small object clearly in a darkened room is to get the image

A. focused on the optic nerve
B. focused in the region of the fovea
C. where the cones are most dense
D. where the rods are most dense
E. focused on the optic chiasm/chiasma

34. The best definition of an illusion is that it is

A. uncertainty as to the facts of the stimulus situation
B. the masking of one sense by another
C. the conflict of one perception with an objective measurement
D. the failure of one sensation to render an accurate picture of the world
E. none of the above

35. A mother who resented her child without being aware of it, yet displays excessive concern and devotion, might be said to be exhibiting a

A. defensive posture
B. displacement
C. repressive malfunction
D. fixation
E. reaction formation

36. Loss of appetite is termed

A. hyperphagia
B. phenylpyavia
C. uralagnia
D. anorexia
E. hypophagia

37. Studies on "cafeteria feeding" of infants, in which they are allowed to eat anything they like over a period of several weeks, indicate that

A. the infants chose mostly sweets and starches and avoided proteins and vegetables
B. the infants tended to choose only milk and other high-protein foods
C. the infants tended to avoid foods with a high vitamin content
D. the infants ate quite a well-balanced diet
E. the infants chose high-vitamin content foods

38. One way in which a teacher can facilitate the learning of concepts is to

A. concentrate upon producing all possible transfer
B. use a concrete approach to teach an abstract concept
C. present all relevant information very gradually, in piecemeal fashion
D. use all of the above methods
E. decrease proactive inhibition

39. The telephone theory proposes that pitch is determined by

A. the frequency of impulses
B. the place stimulated
C. the intensity of stimulation
D. the resting cochlear potential
E. the amplitude of impulses

40. "Extensional" meaning refers to

A. meaning that can be conveyed by pointing to objects or events
B. a synonym for intentional meaning
C. the private meaning that words have for many persons suffering from a mental disorder
D. the logical meaning of a syllogism
E. subjective meaning

41. An individual is less likely to solve a problem if he has

A. practice in trial and error learning
B. a motive to complete the problem
C. a habit which was previously used to solve problems
D. high achievement motive
E. high level of aspiration

42. The optimum time for imprinting ducklings is

A. 15 hours after birth
B. 2 days after birth
C. one week after birth
D. one month after birth
E. 1 hour after birth

43. A person may quickly become oblivious to the feeling of a slightly tight belt around his waist. The best term for this is

A. hortatory percipience
B. subliminal perception
C. assimilation
D. contrast
E. adaptation

44. The first emotions expressed by infants are

A. pleasure and anger
B. fear and euphoria
C. pain and rage
D. anger and fear
E. delight and distress

45. The average infant can sit alone at age

A. one month
B. three months
C. seven months
D. eleven months
E. twelve months

46. The correlation of an infant's intelligence with the speed of his motor development is

A. strongly positive
B. slightly positive
C. essentially zero
D. slightly negative
E. strongly negative

47. The perception of apparent movement is called

A. asch phenomenon
B. motion constancy
C. retinal disparity
D. optical taxis
E. phi-phenomenon

48. A person with an I. Q. of 132 on the new revised version of the Stanford-Binet would have a score

    A. two standard deviations above the mean
    B. twelve standard deviations above the mean
    C. at the mean
    D. one standard deviation below the mean
    E. one standard deviation above the mean

49. Mongolism is associated with

    A. cultural deprivation
    B. pre-natal nutrition
    C. mental ability of the parents
    D. post-natal nutrition
    E. age of the mother

50. Unlike the parents of children with slight mental retardation, parents of children with extreme retardation are likely to be

    A. severely retarded themselves
    B. slightly retarded
    C. of average ability
    D. of superior ability
    E. of slightly better than average ability

51. Phenomenology, dissonance theory, and Gestalt psychology are similar in that

    A. they all predict behavior on the basis of cognitive structure, rather than on the basis of response tendencies
    B. they are all primarily concerned with the establishment of associations between stimuli and responses
    C. they all rest on a contiguity theory rather than a reinforcement theory
    D. they all discourage artificial laboratory experiments as a means of investigating psychological relationships
    E. they all stress the notion of reinforcement

52. The tendency of gaps in a figure to be filled in by the perceiver is called

    A. closure
    B. prägnanz
    C. phi phenomenon
    D. normalization
    E. organization

53. Psychophysics is the study of

    A. the way nerves conduct
    B. the forces acting on the brain which cause the organism to respond one way or another
    C. the relationship between physiological functioning and behavior
    D. the relationship between physical stimuli and sensations
    E. sensory physiology

54. Which one of the following is not an average?

    A. arithmetic mean
    B. range
    C. mode
    D. median
    E. geometric mean

55. A person whose behavior was characterized by expressions of guilt and suicide tendencies and who felt chronically depressed and worthless would be said to be suffering from

    A. paranoia
    B. schizophrenia
    C. neuralgia
    D. an obsessive-compulsive neurosis
    E. an affective disorder

56. Schizophrenia is best described as a condition of personality which

    A. shows frequent and extreme changes in mood or temperament
    B. lacks organizational strength
    C. has never developed adequately
    D. has regressed to the oedipal stage of development
    E. has regressed to the oral stage of development

57. Which of the following conditions indicates an hysterial sympton?

    A. blindness in a person with normal eyes
    B. trembling in a person after an automobile accident
    C. crying in a man after the death of his mother
    D. shrieking by a person taking part in a primitive rite
    E. none of the above

58. The sum of the deviations about the arithmetic mean

    A. is negative
    B. is equal to zero
    C. is equal to the standard deviation
    D. is a weighted average
    E. is left skewed

59. The polygraph measures

    A. brain waves
    B. the truthfulness of an individual
    C. heart rate, respiration rate, perspiration rate
    D. enuresis
    E. hyperphagia

60. An experiment in psychophysics, in which three independent variables were manipulated, with two levels on each; and in which the dependent variable could be measured by an interval scale, would best employ as a statistical technique for analyzing the results

    A. factor analysis
    B. multiple regression
    C. partial correlation
    D. chi-square
    E. analysis of variance

61. The most precise sampling technique is

    A. quota sampling
    B. random sampling
    C. biased sampling
    D. purposive sampling
    E. stratified random sampling

62. The theory of statistical regression would predict that

    A. fathers of short stature are likely to have somewhat taller sons
    B. fathers of average height are likely to have sons who are somewhat shorter
    C. a certain proportion of the population will exhibit atavistic behavior
    D. every individual will return to a previous psychosexual level at some point in his life
    E. a certain proportion of the population will exhibit repressed behavior

63. A study which followed a group of subjects over a period of several years would be a

    A. biographical study
    B. historical study
    C. cross-cultural study
    D. cross-sectional study
    E. longitudinal study

64. Von Frisch in his study of bees, found that they

    A. actually have no means of communicating with one another
    B. use their highly developed sense of smell to find their way back to the hive
    C. can communicate the location of food by means of a dance
    D. can find their way back to the hive even when they are trapped in a box for a few hours
    E. have excellent vision

65. "The number of observations which fall at one point or within a given range on a measurement scale," is a definition of

    A. distribution
    B. epidemic data
    C. incidence
    D. frequency
    E. standard deviation

66. In Kelley's longitudinal study of certain traits over a 20 year period, it was shown that

A. values were least stable
B. vocational interests were least stable
C. attitudes were most stable
D. attitudes were least stable
E. attitudes were more stable than values

67. After two or three days in a sensory deprivation experiment, the typical subject

A. adapts to the situation and begins to find it enjoyable
B. finds the situation unpleasant but is able to think more clearly and concentrate better than he normally could
C. begins to spend 18-22 hours sleeping each day
D. develops symptoms resembling serious mental disorder and refuses to continue
E. develops good categorizing ability

68. The fact that a "pecking order" develops in barnyard fowls indicates that they have

A. an affiliation need
B. a security drive
C. constant hunger drive
D. a status motive
E. need for achievement

69. A change in the sensitivity of a sense organ due to stimulation or lack of stimulation is called

A. alarm reaction
B. homeostasis
C. adaptation
D. anoxia
E. anorexia

70. Eidetic imagery

A. is highly correlated with intelligence
B. is negatively correlated with intelligence
C. is more common among adults than children
D. is more common among children than adults
E. is correlated with perceptual defense

71. The physiological basis of dyslexia may, according to recent research, be associated with

A. unilateral representation of spatial functions in the cerebral hemispheres
B. bilateral representation of spatial functions in the cerebral hemispheres
C. apraxia
D. agraphia and alexia
E. aphasia

Answer questions 72 and 73 with reference to the passage quoted below.

As far back as 1936 surgeons were working out a way to treat a psychosis by an operation called prefrontal lobotomy--the last resort for schizophrenics and manic-depressives. Using a technique devised by the University of Lisbon's emeritus professor Dr. Antonio Caetano de Abreu Freire Egas Moniz, skilled neuro-surgeons cut away important nerve connections in the prefrontal brain lobe (a seat of reasoning) and the thalamus in the rear of the brain (a way station for emotional responses). The operation's aim: helping the patient to a better adjustment with his environment.
Working in a similar field was a 68-year-old Swiss physiologist, Dr. Walter Rudolph Hess, Director of Zurich University's Physiological Institute. A specialist in the circulatory and nervous systems, Dr. Hess studied the reaction of animals to electric shocks. By applying electrodes to parts of a cat's brain he was able to make the animal do what it would normally do if it saw a dog, i.e., hiss, etc. By experiments, Dr. Hess was able to determine how parts of the brain control organs of the body.

72. As a result of a prefrontal lobotomy, doctors hope

A. to eliminate schizophrenia
B. regenerate injured nerve tissue
C. destroy germs which cause the disease
D. cut away important nerve tissue
E. to help the patient get along better in his normal life

73. The operation is based on the theory that

A. people react to electric shock
B. certain parts of the brain control certain types of action
C. adjustment is a matter of proper reactions
D. a cat will hiss if certain spots are touched with an electric wire
E. none of these

74. A figure frequently used in measurements of visual acuity is the

A. Landolt ring
B. Gordon arrow
C. Neiman illusion
D. Cowan polygon
E. London chain

75. The total number of senses possessed by the normal human

A. is known to be five
B. is usually taken as the number of different kinds of sense receptors
C. is equal to the number of sensory trunks in the cortex
D. is not accurately characterized in any of these ways
E. is known to be six

76. The "extinguishing" of a learned response

A. requires the withholding of reinforcement
B. refers to the complete eradication or unlearning of that response
C. is best achieved by means of a mild punishment
D. may be characterized in all of the above ways
E. is done most quickly after partial reinforcement

77. Which should be regarded as the most enduring and constructive type of extrinsic motivation for learning?

A. social approval from the group
B. self-approval for right responses
C. praise or blame given by an individual in authority
D. symbols or tokens (e.g. high marks) which indirectly lead to other rewards
E. peer-group approval

78. From the standpoint of Skinnerian theory, the chief value of the teaching machine is its

A. greater amount of reinforcement
B. making it clear exactly what the stimulus is
C. control of what is reinforced
D. elimination of human interaction from the learning process
E. producing learning in large steps

79. If obtained GRE scores are ranked in order from the highest to the lowest, the exact middle score is the

A. median
B. standard score
C. mid-point
D. mode
E. mean

80. Which of the following sequences of events would be a cue to the experimenter that conditioning had taken place? (UCS = unconditioned stimulus, CS = conditioned stimulus, CR = conditioned response)

A. UCS-CS-CR
B. CR-CS-UCS
C. CS-UCS-CR
D. CS-CR-UCS
E. none of the above

81. Psychologists are generally agreed that the term "instinct" is capable of explaining

A. human tropisms
B. the biological roots of all human behavior

C. behavior like food intake and sexual behavior
D. all of the behavior of organisms below mammals
E. only a small portion of human behavior

82. Shivering, eating, and perspiring are all instances of

A. kinesthesis
B. homeostasis
C. dissociative reactions
D. compensation
E. neurasthenia

83. If the median, mode and mean, all fall at the same point, the distribution is likely to be

A. normal
B. skewed
C. nominal
D. ratio
E. ordinate

84. Which of the following would the trend line most closely resemble when plotted on graph paper?

A. circle
B. straight line
C. curved line
D. symmetrical distribution
E. left skewed distribution

85. With reference to the correlation coefficient, which one of the following statement is true?

A. The closer the points on a scatter diagram are clustered around the regression line used for the estimating of the dependent variable, the higher the <u>absolute value</u> of the correlation coefficient.
B. The closer the points on a scatter diagram are clustered around the regression line used for estimating of the dependent variable, the higher the <u>value</u> of the correlation coefficient.
C. The correlation coefficient ranges from 0 to +1.
D. The correlation coefficient can be determined by examining the scatter diagram.
E. The sign of the correlation coefficient bears no relationship to the slope of the regression line.

86. An individual plans to become a doctor. However, he is flunking out of high school, and has a borderline mentally retarded IQ. His anxiety is most probably caused by

A. inferiority feelings because of his IQ
B. incongruence between actual experience and the ideal self
C. birth trauma
D. insecurity regarding his future
E. denying significant visceral feelings to conscious awareness

87. The personality test which is sometimes jokingly referred to as "the sane man's MMPI" is

A. Gough's CPI
B. Edwards Inventory
C. Lowenfeld Mosaic Test
D. Taylor's MAS
E. Crowne-Marlowe Scale

88. Data from the New Haven studies of mental illness by Hollingshead and Radlich seem to show that psychosis is more prevalent

A. in New Haven than in other cities that have been studied
B. among the lower classes than among the upper classes
C. today than 50 years ago
D. in urban than in rural areas
E. in rural than in urban areas

89. The most effective therapy for alcoholism is

A. shock therapy
B. narcoanalysis
C. psychoanalysis
D. active membership in Alcoholics Anonymous
E. Skinnerian therapy

90. Group therapy, as seen by psychoanalytic theorists, has the advantage that

  A. multiple transference can take place
  B. regression is less likely
  C. a more direct observation of super-ego formation may be made
  D. therapy is obtained for a lower cost
  E. repression is lessened more quickly

91. Experiments on group behavior indicate that deviates from the group norm

  A. are rejected by the group purely because they disagree
  B. are neither rejected nor accepted any more than any other group member
  C. are generally accepted more because they display leadership qualities
  D. are rare in our society
  E. are always accepted by the group

92. Experiments on esthetics have demonstrated that works of art are most pleasing when

  A. a completely unpredictable pattern is formed with familiar elements
  B. a completely predictable pattern is formed with unfamiliar elements
  C. a somewhat predictable pattern is formed with largely familiar elements
  D. a barely predictable pattern is formed with elements which are unfamiliar
  E. an unpredictable pattern is formed with unfamiliar elements

93. Experiments in which stooges give incorrect responses about their perceptions in order to get subjects to agree with them have been performed by

  A. Hovland
  B. Sherif
  C. Kraft-Ebbing
  D. Allport
  E. Asch

94. Attitude-change studies have found that the relationship between the fearsomeness of the communication and the amount of attitude change produced is

  A. curvilinear, with slightly frightening ones more effective
  B. curvilinear, with slightly frightening ones less effective
  C. linear--the more frightening, the more effective
  D. linear--the more frightening, the less effective
  E. none of the above

95. Attempts to persuade audiences by means of "subliminal" messages

  A. have proved to be highly effective
  B. generally sell more of a product than regular direct sales techniques
  C. have generally supported the stimulus-response model of human behavior
  D. are not accurately characterized in any of these ways
  E. have been more effective on television than in movies

96. Descriptive statistics and inferential statistics differ in that

  A. descriptive statistics are usually more detailed and exacting in nature and format than are inferential statistics
  B. descriptive statistics are less apt to be numerical in nature and format than are inferential statistics
  C. descriptive statistics describe the population while inferential statistics are used to make inferences about the population
  D. all of the above
  E. none of the above

97. Which of the following statistical tests provides a derivation of "p"?

A. t-test
B. chi-square test
C. correlation analysis
D. F test
E. all of the above

98. Learning which is said to occur without incentives and without reward is generally called

A. unmotivated retention
B. non-reinforced acquisition
C. incidental learning
D. cortical-drive learning
E. partially reinforced learning

99. Monocular cues for depth perception

A. are illustrated by the phenomenon of "retinal disparity"
B. refer to cues that require only one eye
C. require two eyes for the effect --but act upon each eye individually
D. play a dominant role only when the light receptors are omatidia
E. are illustrated by the phi phenomenon

100. Signal detection is usually concerned with

A. echoic elaboration
B. vigilance
C. subliminal perception
D. eidetic imagery
E. day dreaming

101. The principle that two events must be closely related temporally and spatially if they are to be associated in learning is the

A. principle of polarity
B. law of organization
C. principle of nearness
D. law of contact
E. law of contiguity

102. Skinner's typical measure of the course of learning in rats was

A. magnitude of response
B. number of correct associations with the stimulus
C. mean number of responses per minute
D. cumulative responses over time
E. amplitude of response

103. The term "non-parametric statistics" refers to a variety of statistical procedures which

A. require at least an interval scale if their use is to be valid
B. make no assumptions regarding the form of the population-distribution
C. deal only with scores which can be ranked in magnitude from least to greatest
D. make no assumptions about the reliability of the data
E. require normally distributed data

104. A gradual drop in a performance curve might be indicative of several different occurrences. These would include

A. inhibition, classical conditioning, negative transfer
B. infavoidance, prohibition, negative transfer
C. inhibition, fatigue, extinction
D. prohibition, extinction, redirection
E. inhibition, prohibition, redirection

105. The best definition of human engineering is that it is concerned with

A. providing therapy with physical methods
B. the design of equipment and tasks performed in the operation of equipment
C. the alteration of genetic structure by chemical means
D. the application of computers and scientific measuring instruments to the betterment of human society
E. automated instruction methods

106. One of the applied uses of content analysis during World War II was

A. determination of the propagandist nature of questionable literature
B. the treatment of shell-shock and other war neuroses
C. the rapid statistical analysis of personality tests administered at military induction
D. assistance in scoring analytically the material in projective tests
E. quick determination of intelligence functions of draftees

107. The best evidence indicates that neurosis is largely

A. a learned reaction to stress and frustration
B. evidence of a congenital weakness
C. the usual precursor of phychosis
D. a form of malingering
E. correlated with low intelligence

108. "Functional psychosis" may best be defined as

A. a psychosis which is assumed to be uncaused by organic damage or disease of the brain
B. a psychosis caused by the failure of certain nervous pathways to perform properly
C. a psychosis which is induced experimentally in laboratory animals
D. a psychosis of indefinitely long duration
E. a psychosis of rapid onset

109. That form of schizophrenia which is characterized by childish and regressed behavior is called

A. catatonic
B. affective
C. paranoid
D. retrograde
E. hebephrenic

110. A mental disturbance in which the individual is excited and elated without any apparent reason is called

A. hypomania
B. dypsomania
C. orthomania
D. pyromania
E. hypermania

111. The most important source of frustration for human beings is

A. obstacles in the environment
B. personal inadequacy
C. goals which cannot be reached
D. motivational conflict
E. high need achievement

112. The physiological reaction to stress which is characterized by an alarm reaction, resistance to stress and eventual exhaustion is called

A. general-adaptation syndrome
B. stress-reaction pattern
C. dynamic-adjustment sequence
D. steroid-output paradigm
E. assimilation-adaptation sequence

113. The region at the base of the brain which is intimately involved in most emotional and physiological motivation is the

A. medulla
B. pineal body
C. rhinencephalon
D. pituitary gland
E. hypothalamus

114. Rigid behavior developed by frequent reinforcement or as a result of frustration is called

A. inhibition
B. maladaptation
C. fixation
D. response decrement
E. reaction formation

115. The best definition of "meaning," in a psychological sense, is that it is

A. implicit muscle response
B. a portion of a response usually elicited by another stimulus
C. an identity of two stimuli
D. a form of trial-and-error learning
E. none of the above

116. Nonsense words

A. become more "meaningful" as their statistical properties approach those of English
B. are learned more rapidly than those which evoke too many associations
C. are seldom used in psychological experiments
D. were first compiled in the Thorndike-Lorge List
E. cannot be remembered more than 22 hours

117. The period in creative thinking in which the individual is not actively thinking about the problem and unconscious processes are permitted to work on it is called

A. introspection
B. invagination
C. infra-processing
D. gestation
E. incubation

118. The process of learning to solve problems of the same general type with greater and greater facility is called

A. facilitation
B. learning set
C. retroactive transfer
D. insight
E. proactive transfer

119. In order to compensate for the serial-position effect when memorizing a poem, it would be wise to spend more time studying

A. the first part
B. the middle part
C. the last part
D. the first and last parts
E. both the middle and last parts

120. A teacher would probably best motivate a student to contribute pertinent, informative comments to a class discussion by

A. praising the student every time he makes a worthwhile contribution
B. reproving the student every time he makes a worthless contribution
C. occasionally praising the student when he makes a worthwhile contribution
D. occasionally reproving the student when he makes a worthless contribution
E. never reproving the student when he makes a worthless contribution

121. The belief that the study of mathematics and Latin is useful because it improves general thinking ability is called

A. formal discipline theory
B. cognitive advancement theory
C. basic studies hypothesis
D. progressive education theory
E. logical theorist hypothesis

122. All of the statements about <u>retinal sensitivity</u> below are true, EXCEPT

A. average background luminance is detected by receptor cells
B. luminance in surrounding regions is mediated by horizontal cells
C. changes in space and time are mediated by amacrine cells at bipolar cell terminals
D. ganglion cells also react to change by amplifying the amplitudes of amacrine cell responses
E. amacrine and ganglion cells together create a concentric, antagonistic receptive field, tending to reduce the response amplitude of ganglionic cells

123. Skinner believes that the proper approach to the study of behavior is

A. to construct detailed hypothesis before beginning laboratory work
B. to base theories of behavior closely on their physiological underpinnings
C. to rest behavioral theory primarily on the notion of the "conceptual nervous system"
D. to avoid undue theorizing and "physiologizing"
E. a deductive theory

124. The first occurrence of an operant behavior

A. is best explained by Gestalt theorists
B. is not adequately accounted for by Hullian drive-reduction theory
C. occurs at the age of about 8 months
D. is a response to a clearly defined external stimulus
E. is best explained by Miller and Dollard

125. The term in modern social theory which most closely approximates Freud's concept of ego-ideal is

A. sociometric choice
B. role model
C. father-figure
D. preferred self
E. none of the above

126. The chronological order of Freud's psychosexual levels is

A. latent, oral, anal, genital, phallic
B. latent, genital, anal, phallic, oral
C. oral, anal, genital, phallic, latent
D. oral, anal, phallic, latent, genital
E. anal, genital, oral, latent, phallic

127. In Freud's psychoanalytic scheme, dreams are assumed to be

A. evidence of a deep-rooted psychopathology
B. repressed sexual feelings
C. the expression of a wish
D. struggles between the id and the super-ego
E. struggles between the id and ego

128. We have computed the value of chi-square for a 12-cell table. To find the probability that the data-configuration found occurred by chance, we go into a table of the values of chi-square with ________ degrees of freedom.

A. 6 B. 5
C. 11 D. 12
E. cannot be determined

129. The rank-order correlation co-efficient between people's scores on the California F-scale and the inverses of their scores is ________.

A. exactly 1
B. less than 1, but 0 or greater
C. less than 0, but greater than -1
D. exactly -1
E. cannot be determined

130. The term "paradoxical cold" refers to

A. the cold sensation one gets from certain auditory experiences
B. the sensation of warmth produced by a cold stimulus
C. the sensation of coldness produced by a warm stimulus
D. the lowering of body temperatures following prolonged exposure to certain high-saturation colors
E. both A and C

131. The Purkinje effect is

A. observed when colors are mixed in unequal proportions
B. produced when an image falls on the blind spot

C. the name for loss of eyesight accompanying age
D. explained by the differential sensitivity of the rods and cones at various places along the spectrum
E. produced when an image falls on the fovea

132. Most color-blind people

A. are tritanopes
B. are women
C. can't tell when the traffic light is green
D. confuse two colors
E. have excellent night vision

133. An experiment on cats in which the animals were allowed to sleep but were prevented from dreaming (by awakening them whenever an electroencephalogram indicated the brain waves typical of dreaming) showed that

A. the cats developed serious mental disorders and eventually died
B. there was no effect on the behavior of the cats
C. the cats preferred dreamless sleep to sleep interrupted by dreams
D. the cats became more alert and more capable of learning
E. the cats became better in operant learning situations

134. Which of the following would be the best activity to engage in after studying for an important examination?

A. studying some related subject
B. reading lecture notes for an entirely different course
C. reading a novel
D. going to sleep
E. reviewing the same subject

135. A difficulty with the plotting of average, rather than individual group curves, is the following:

A. average curves are statistically unreliable
B. average curves do not show variations from individual to individual
C. average curves do not reflect the course of development for any individual
D. both A and B
E. both B and C

136. Vectors in a psychological field

A. refer to people or ideas
B. are frequently used to describe the activity of the sense receptors
C. were used in the work of Weber and Fechner
D. represent forces acting on an individual or group
E. are synonymous with valences

137. A basic tenet of Gestalt psychology is that

A. dynamic factors in retention are more important than those due to set
B. positive structure have greater regularity than negative structure
C. things are perceived differently when they appear in different contexts
D. all of the above
E. absolute shape of elements determines perception

138. Retroactive inhibition : memory trace

A. proactive inhibition : retention curve
B. negative transfer : task to be learned
C. proactive inhibition : cell assembly
D. negative transfer : task already learned
E. proactive inhibition : task to be learned

139. Most studies in which maturation factors were co-varied with practice have shown that

A. practice has no effect at all on the emergent behavior patterns

B. the function will appear without any practice
C. practice improves the functioning
D. none of the above is true
E. B and C are true

140. If one member of a pair of twins is given extensive practice in some function, while the other member is restricted, the experimental methodology employed is called

A. matched sampling
B. co-twin control
C. hereditary control
D. environmental control
E. none of the above

Answer questions 141-142 with reference to the passage quoted below.

A psychologist wishes to study the extent of transfer of training from Task A to Task B. He has subjects perform Task A and then perform Task B. This group of subjects is the experimental group.

141. If the psychologist found that performance of Task A made it more difficult to learn Task B, it could be said that the effect of A on B was:

A. retroactive facilitation
B. proactive fibrillation
C. retroactive fibrillation
D. retroactive inhibition
E. proactive inhibition

142. If the psychologist wished to determine whether the performance of Task B led to retroactive inhibition of Task A, he would have subjects

A. perform A, rest, perform B
B. perform A, perform B, perform A
C. perform B, perform A, perform B
D. perform B, perform activity X, perform A
E. perform A, perform activity X, perform B

143. The psychological role of G. H. Mead's "generalized other" is similar to that of

A. displacement
B. the "looking-glass self"
C. the ego
D. the superego
E. projection

In questions 144-145 you are to identify the name or designation which is not appropriately grouped with the others.

144. A. hysteria
B. amnesia
C. dissociative reaction
D. fugue
E. aphasia

145. A. resonance theory
B. dissonance theory
C. frequency theory
D. volley-place theory
E. Von Bekesy's theory

Answer questions 146-147 with reference to the passage quoted below.

An insurance company wishes to set up a testing procedure to use in its selection of salesman. They wish to use as criteria of the tests (1) how much insurance is sold by the new salesman in his first six months and (2) whether or not the salesman is still with the company after one year. A psychologist is hired as a consultant. Assuming the psychologist is competent in the area of tests and measurement, answer the following questions about his probably advice to the company:

146. The psychologist is likely to recommend for the selection procedure the use of

A. a psychiatric interview and a non-verbal I.Q. test
B. an autobiographical statement and a vocational interest questionnaire
C. the Rorschach test and the MMPI
D. the Bender-Gestalt test and the TAT
E. Gough's CPI and the MMPI

147. If the psychologist wishes to obtain a correlation between one of his tests and the dichotomous criterion of whether the salesman remains with the company or not, he will probably use

A. Kendall's Tau
B. Spearman Rho
C. Coefficient Alpha
D. Kendall's Zeta
E. Biserial correlation

Answer questions 148-149-150 with reference to the chart below.

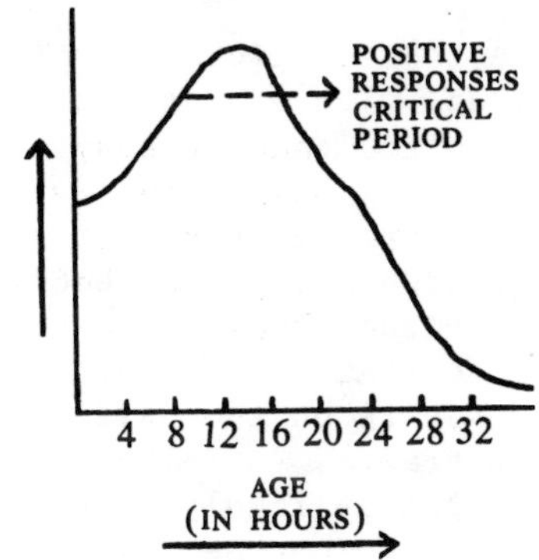

148. The peak of the graph shown above (the critical period) refers to

A. that time when the organism's visual sensitivity is determined
B. the crucial time for the development of motor activity
C. the time when exposure to a mother object will most effect the organism's social behavior
D. the time when exposure to a mother object will most effect the organism's perceptual abilities
E. none of the above

149. Imprinting differs from discrimination learning in that

A. primacy produces better discrimination learning and recency produces better imprinting
B. recency produces better discrimination learning and primacy produces better imprinting
C. discrimination learning is not differentially effected by primacy vs recency, while imprinting behavior <u>is</u>
D. imprinting is not effected by primacy vs. recency, while discrimination learning <u>is</u>
E. none of the above is true

150. It has been found that, as the critical period comes to an end,

A. fear increases
B. fear decreases
C. level of fear remains unchanged
D. both A and C may occur
E. both B and C may occur

Answer questions 151-152 with reference to the chart below.

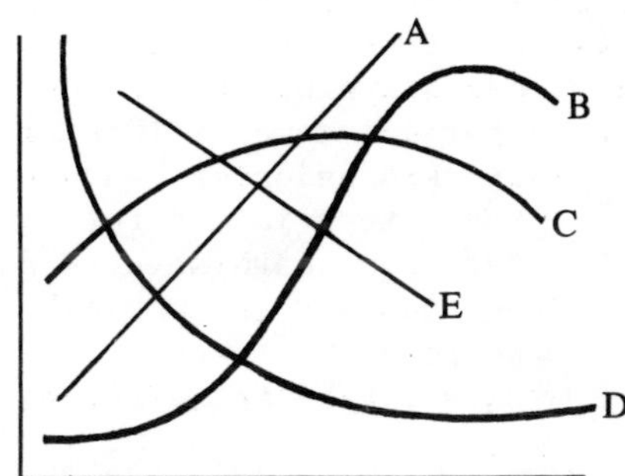

Choose the function, A, B, C, D, or E, to which each of the following best applies:

151. The function which represents a nonmonotonic relationship.

152. The function relating sensation to simulus intensity, if a narrow middle range of stimuli is represented along the abscissa.

Answer questions 153-154 with reference to the passage quoted below.

An experiment employing rats as subjects used the following procedure: On ten different occasions a rat was placed in a white box and given electric shock for 60 seconds. At the end of the shock period, a door was raised and the rat was allowed to escape into a neighboring black box where no shock was present. Following this, whenever the rat was placed into the white box it would escape immediately into the black box. In fact, even though it had received no shock in the white box since the original ten trials, the rat was capable of learning several procedures for escaping into the black box, including pressing a lever and turning a wheel.

153. From the standpoint of psychological theory, the most interesting aspect of this experiment is the fact that

A. a rat's fear drive can become conditioned to a stimulus such as a white box
B. a conditioned stimulus such as a white box can serve as a negative incentive motivating new learning
C. it required only 10 sixty-second shock sessions to induce an intense fear in the rat
D. rats can learn several different responses to accomplish the same purpose
E. rats can be motivated by fear

154. This experiment involved two kinds of conditioning. There were

A. classical and pavlovian
B. instrumental and operant
C. classical and instrumental
D. respondent and pavlovian
E. respondent and operant

Answer questions 155-156-157 with reference to the following:

The following table gives the intercorrelations of the original trait scales of the Bernreuter Personality Inventory. The population upon which they are based is a sample of 800 college students.

Intercorrelations of Bernreuter Scores

	Neurotic Tendency	Self-Sufficiency	Introversion	Dominance
Neurotic Tendency		—.38	.89	—.67
Self-Sufficiency			—.33	.52
Introversion				—.62
Dominance				

155. The table indicates that an individual with a high score on the Neurotic Tendency trait is

A. extremely likely to have a high score on the Self-Sufficiency trait
B. extremely likely to have a low score on the Self-Sufficiency trait
C. fairly likely to have a high score on the Self-Sufficiency trait
D. fairly likely to have a low score on the Self-Sufficiency trait
E. likely to have a score in the middle range on the Self-Sufficiency trait

156. Only one-half of the table is filled in. If the other half of the table were completed,

A. it would give the split-half reliabilities of the scales
B. it would give the validities of the scales
C. it would give exactly the same information already conveyed by the table
D. it would give the factor loadings of the scales
E. it would give equivalence reliabilities on the scales.

157. If the reliability of the Self-Sufficiency scale is .80, the

highest validity it could have would be approximately

A. .65
B. .75
C. .40
D. 1.00
E. .90

Answer questions 158-159-160-161 with reference to the passage quoted below.

In his early writings, E. L. Thorndike stated the view that reward would increase the tendency to repeat the behavior it immediately followed and that punishment would decrease the tendency to repeat the behavior. On the basis of later work with both human and animal subjects, however, he revised this view and reached the conclusion that punishment had no inherently weakening effect on behavior. In one experiment, subjects unfamiliar with Spanish were asked to guess the meaning of a Spanish word from 5 alternatives. The reward was the word "right" from the experimenter, and punishment the word "wrong." As expected, reward increased the probability that a response would be repeated on a second trial (the probability was considerably greater than the chance 20%) but punishment did not decrease the probability below the chance level of 20%. With punishment, in fact, the probability of repetition remained above 20% by a considerable amount.

158. Thorndike's earlier view on reward and punishment has been called

A. The Reinforcement Principle
B. The Pleasure-Pain Principle
C. Drive-alteration theory
D. The Law of Effect
E. Hedonistic theory

159. Thorndike based his view on the ineffectiveness of punishment partly on the fact that

A. punishment gives much less information than reward
B. punishment is immoral
C. organisms like reward more than they dislike punishment
D. individuals can easily repress the effects of punishment
E. not all organisms are susceptible to punishment

160. The experimental finding which would be most damaging to Thorndike's view that punishment is ineffective would be

A. the finding that reward for correct responses to Spanish words had only a very slight effect of increasing the probability that the response would be repeated on a second trial
B. the finding that, in the absence of either reward or punishment on the first trial, the probability of repeating an incorrect response is considerably higher than 20%
C. the finding that subjects could learn the correct meaning of Spanish words only with great difficulty
D. the finding that rats are capable of learning a lever press response more quickly if they are not punished for incorrect responses
E. none of the above

161. Later revisions of Thorndike's views have emphasized that punishment can be effective only if

A. it is severe
B. it is accompanied by reward
C. some response other than the punished one is available
D. the punishment is always administered whenever the response takes place
E. it is mild

Answer questions 162-163 with reference to the passage quoted below.

"One area of research in which prejudices have operated to prevent progress is the question of the size of the unit to be studied. There is widespread confusion of the goal of scientific accuracy with the technique of measuring the smallest possible units. Thus a study in child development may concern itself largely with time units of a fraction of a second ('reflex withdrawal of hand', reaction of the eyelid). In fact, however, objective measurements are frequently as readily obtained when the unit is very large as when it is miniscule. The larger unit indeed is often preferable to the smaller. It is simply not feasible to describe the movements of a star by describing the movement of every particle contained in it."

162. The author would most likely approve, as a tool of psychological research

A. the study of reflex behavior in lower organisms
B. the use of observer rating scales to determine cohesiveness of a group
C. the use of lever-press responses as an indication of learning
D. the use of Rorschach protocols in child development research
E. measurement of consummatory behavior after food deprivation in rats.

163. The author's thinking is most akin to that of

A. behaviorists
B. introspectionists
C. skinnerians
D. drive-reduction theorists
E. Gestalt theorists

164. Which one of the following is not, strictly speaking, one of Freud's stages of psychosexual development?

A. genital
B. oral
C. Oedipal
D. phallic
E. anal

165. Otto Klineberg, in a study of children of Negroes who had migrated from the South to the North, discovered that their measured I.Q. (intelligence test score)

A. increased for a period, then remained increased
B. increased for a period, then returned to about the original level
C. stayed about the same
D. decreased for a period, then returned to about the original level
E. decreased for a period, then remained depressed

166. The authoritarian personality is not characterized by

A. an introspective nature
B. conformity to societal mores
C. a superstitious bent
D. a tendency to suppress his imagination
E. none of the above

Answer questions 167-168-169 with reference to the three tables on the following page.

167. Table 3 shows

A. no relation
B. a strong relation
C. it is impossible to tell without more information
D. a weak relation
E. the situation is impossible

168. In order to fill in Table 1, one needs

A. the rest of the marginals
B. one more cell entry
C. no more information
D. two more cell entries
E. the total number of cases

169. The correct number of cases in the fourth cell of Table 3 is

A. impossible to determine
B. 6
C. 10
D. 9
E. 12

Answer questions 170-171-172 with reference to the passage quoted below.

An experiment by Miller involved shocking a rat in the presence of another rat. After several such episodes the rat receiving the shock began to attack the other rat. When the "bystander" rat was replaced by a doll, the shocked rat attacked it also.

170. Inasmuch as the goal of the shocked rat--to stop the shock--was unobtainable, its behavior can be viewed as an instance of the

Below are three tables and a series of questions about them.

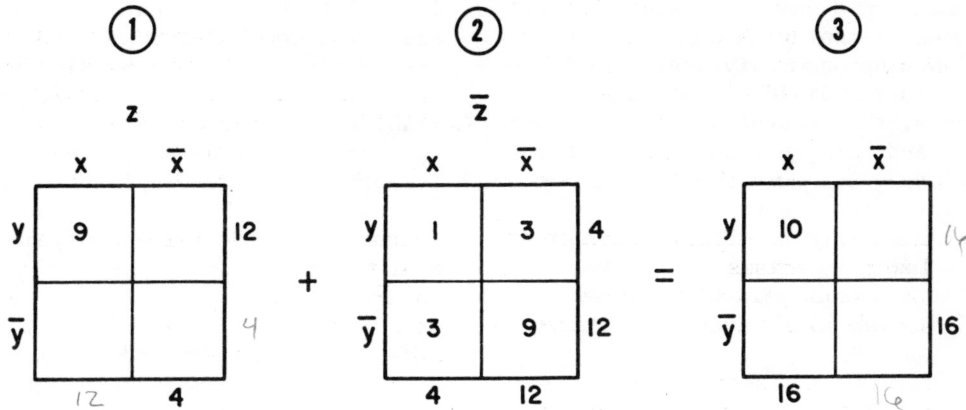

A. frustration-aggression hypothesis
B. frustration-regression hypothesis
C. goal-gradient hypothesis
D. goal-regression hypothesis
E. approach-approach hypothesis

171. The generalization of the attacking response to the bystander rat onto the doll is an instance of

A. stimulus generalization
B. response generalization
C. aggression-compensation
D. anticipatory goal response
E. displacement

172. The experiment could be considered an experimental analogue of the phenomenon of

A. sublimation
B. reaction-formation
C. fixation
D. projection
E. displacement

Answer questions 173-174-175 with reference to the passage quoted below.

Higher psychological functions can be seen to grow out of biological mechanisms. The adaptation level of the organism is a balance between its assimilation and accommodation; adaptation tends toward equilibrium. In adaptation, the child learns to control shifts of orientation, and he further develops what we will call "operations."

173. Assimilation refers to

A. the modification that the organism makes on the environment
B. the modification that the environment makes on the organism
C. the learning of new concepts
D. the interaction between the environment and the organism
E. none of the above

174. Operations, as defined in the paragraph, are

A. overt actions
B. research methodologies
C. actions which have been internalized
D. groupable into relational systems which influence concept formation
E. both C and D

175. The "groups" of operations which fulfill conditions of reversibility and combinatoriality are most similar to

A. Bruner's strategies
B. Hull's fractional anticipatory goal responses
C. Hovland's positive and negative instances
D. Tolman's expectancies
E. Skinner's superstitious behavior

Answer questions 176-177-178 with reference to the passage quoted below.

A recent experiment with college students involved asking one individual to tell a lie to another individual. In one group of subjects, the student was paid $1 for his lie. Another group received $20. Later all subjects were questioned regarding the extent to which their own beliefs had shifted in the direction of the lie which they had told. It was found that students paid $1 for the lie believed it more afterwards than students paid $20.

176. This experiment would most likely have been conducted to test

A. assimilation-contrast theory
B. Piaget's notions about the development of morality
C. hypotheses about appropriate pay scales in industry
D. cognitive dissonance theory
E. POX theory

177. No differences in beliefs regarding the lie would likely have been obtained if

A. the subjects had been well acquainted with the person to whom they told the lie
B. the subjects had been required to tell the lie instead of requested to do so
C. the subjects had had better-developed moral values
D. the experimenter had contrasted the subjects' practices with their beliefs
E. the subjects were more honest

178. The dependent variable was

A. the amount paid for the lie
B. the extent to which the subject believed his lie
C. whether or not the subject told the lie
D. not measured
E. how believable the lie was

Answer questions 179-180 with reference to the following passage.

A recent technique which has been extensively applied in the field of psychological testing is that of factor analysis. This method attempts to discover the meaning of a test by discovering and exploring its correlation with other variables. Factor analysis has been used in studying psychometric measures of interests, abilities, aptitudes and personality. In the end, the result of a factor analysis will be largely dependent on the outlook of the psychologist performing the study. While factor analysis is a mathematical technique, the psychologist will organize and label his results so that they are most meaningful to him.

179. Factor analysis tries to determine

A. the distinct abilities which a test measures
B. the overlap between different tests supposedly measuring the same quantity
C. the possible presence of factors which a test taps only slightly
D. all of the above
E. none of the above

180. One criterion that the final factor analysis should meet is called simple structure. This is met when

A. each test is described in terms of many factors
B. most of the factor loadings are high
C. each test is described in terms of a few factors
D. both A and B are true
E. both A and C are true

181. The statistical methodology which reduces a large number of test scores into a few basic factors is

A. Q-sort
B. factor analysis
C. chi-square
D. T-test
E. rho test

Answer questions 182-183 with reference to the following diagram:

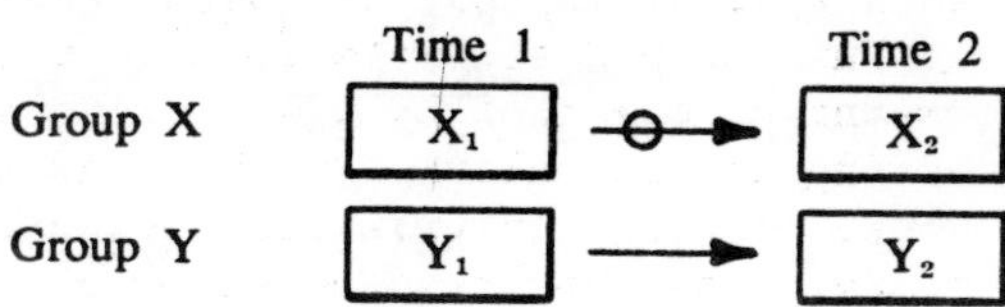

In the diagram above, boxes X_1 and X_2 represent the members of groups X at times 1 and 2, respectively, and boxes Y_1 and Y_2 represent the members of group Y at times 1 and 2.

182. If persons assigned to the two groups randomly and some experimental variation (0) is introduced between X_1 and X_2 , group Y would be considered

 A. an experimental group
 B. a secondary group
 C. a unitary group
 D. a control group
 E. an out-group

183. An ex post facto study of a group of alcoholics in an effort to determine why they became alcoholics would necessarily involve examination of box(es)

 A. X_1 and X_2
 B. X_2 and Y_2
 C. X_1 , X_2 , Y_1 , Y_2
 D. X_2 only
 E. Y_1 only

184. The American psychologist most responsible for the development of factorial methods is

 A. L. L. Thurstone
 B. J. McKeen Cattell
 C. E. L. Thorndike
 D. Estes
 E. Mosteller

Answer questions 185-186-187 with reference to the following passage.

In a recent experiment, subjects were presented with a series of words by a tachistoscopic apparatus. The words were varied so that some were "dirty" or suggestive, while the others were in common usage. It was typically found, at least in the first few of the so-called perceptual defense experiments, that the "dirty" stimuli required higher visual thresholds in order to be correctly reported.

185. The dependent variable in the type of experiment described above is

 A. type of word presented
 B. length of tachistoscopic exposure
 C. the reporting of the presentation of the word by the observer
 D. size of type in which the word is shown
 E. none of the above

186. A psychologist accepting the results presented above would predict that, if hungry and non-hungry subjects were presented with tachistoscopic exposures of food

 A. the recognition threshold would be the same for hungry and non-hungry subjects
 B. the recognition threshold would be lower for hungry subjects
 C. the recognition threshold would be lower for sated subjects
 D. both A and C are true
 E. both A and B are true

187. One of the chief methodological flaws in the early perceptual defense experiments was

 A. the failure to equate for frequency of word occurrence
 B. the use of too homogeneous groups of subjects
 C. the use of too heterogeneous groups of subjects
 D. the failure to equate for vowel equivalency in dirty and neutral words
 E. none of the above

Answer questions 188-189 with reference to the following passage.

Too great stress has been laid upon constitutional factors and early childhood experiences as rigid determinants of personality. We cannot think in this historically deterministic way; man is a social animal. He is motivated by his expectations of the future more than by the experiences and events of the past. It is these goals and beliefs that influence conduct and cause psychological events.

188. The view stated above opposes a view of

A. altruism
B. humanitarianism
C. co-operation
D. determinism
E. awareness

189. Adler's doctrine of the creative self holds that

A. man essentially makes his own personality
B. man does not use all the creative powers available to him
C. man is not innately endowed with creativity; he learns to be creative
D. both A and C are true
E. none of the above is true

In questions 190-191-192, identify the pair which represents an incorrect association.

190. A. Maslow--self-actualization
B. Lewin--field theory
C. Hurvich--opponent colors
D. Harlow--affectional drive
E. Krech--nerve recording

191. A. Guilford--psychometrics
B. Guttman--psychometrics
C. Cronback--psychometrics
D. Festinger--psychometrics
E. Eysenck--psychometrics

192. A. Campbell--multitrait-multimethod matrix
B. Hess--ethology
C. Milgram--obedience
D. Bales--neurobiotaxis
E. Lorenz--ethology

193. Primitive emotions such as fear, rage, strong hunger, or intense sexual desire are closely associated with a functional structure in the brain known as the

A. reticular activating system (RAS)
B. adrenal system
C. pituitary-adrenal system
D. limbic system
E. amygdala

194. Which one of the following is not a psychological defense-mechanism?

A. projection
B. displacement
C. reaction-formation
D. repression
E. alienation

Answer questions 195-196 with reference to the following passage.

A recent study by Ehrlich, Guttman, Schonbach and Mills has shown that owners of a new car read advertisements for their type of car more than for other cars that they had considered buying but did not. They also read ads for cars that they had not considered at all. Moreover, new car purchasers who had considered at least two or more "other" cars were more likely to read advertisements for their new car than were those purchasers who had considered only one other car, or no other cars. The results of this study are considered to bear out several predictions from cognitive dissonance theory.

195. The results of the above study bear out this assumption:

A. persons will seek out consonant information after making a choice which involved rejecting a positively valued alternative
B. persons will seek out information so that they can know which of two positively valued alternatives to reject before making a decision

C. as the number of alternative choices increase, dissonance will increase

D. both A and C
E. both B and C

196. Dissonance theory differs from conflict theory chiefly

A. dissonance relates to post-decisional situations and conflict to pre-decisional ones
B. goals creating dissonance are different from goals creating conflict
C. different relationships between subject and goal pertain in conflict and in dissonance theory
D. dissonance theory allows for stimulus generalization while conflict theory does not
E. both B and C

197. Jung assumes that man's behavior is governed by

A. social instincts
B. biological urges
C. inborn archetypes
D. inborn instincts
E. libido

Answer questions 198-199-200 with reference to the following passage.

The psychologist is interested in human growth functions since changes in human structures are accompanied by changes in function. The analogy holds in behavior. As the human being develops, the psychologist finds it less rewarding to study simple changes in structure; rather, he is more interested in various psychological changes with age, in situations where he either has or has not instituted training procedures. Typically, such studies are either cross-sectional or longitudinal in approach.

198. IQ scores obtained prior to which age listed below are useless in predicting performance during the school years?

A. 18 months
B. 20 months
C. 24 months
D. 30 months
E. 36 months

199. Cross-sectional procedures have been criticized on the grounds of

A. the operation of selective factors in different age groups
B. sample shrinkage
C. use of superior, and therefore unrepresentative samples
D. differences in experiential backgrounds among the different groups
E. both A and D

200. Most physiological growth curves, obtained by testing the same individual in a standard test situation at different ages, are similar to

A. the normal curve
B. learning curves
C. decay of excitation curves
D. positively skewed curves
E. none of the above

SAMPLE TEST 3

ANSWER KEY

1. E
2. D
3. C
4. B
5. A
6. A
7. D
8. D
9. E
10. D
11. E
12. A
13. B
14. A
15. B
16. D
17. A
18. E
19. A
20. D
21. E
22. D
23. D
24. C
25. B
26. C
27. C
28. E
29. C
30. E
31. C
32. C
33. D
34. C
35. E
36. D
37. D
38. B
39. A
40. A
41. C
42. A
43. E
44. E
45. C
46. C
47. E
48. A
49. E
50. C
51. A
52. A
53. D
54. B
55. E
56. B
57. A
58. B
59. C
60. E
61. E
62. A
63. E
64. C
65. D
66. D
67. D
68. D
69. C
70. D
71. B
72. E
73. B
74. A
75. D
76. A
77. B
78. C
79. A
80. D
81. E
82. B
83. A
84. B
85. A
86. B
87. A
88. B
89. D
90. A
91. A
92. C
93. E
94. A
95. D
96. C
97. E
98. C
99. B
100. B
101. E
102. D
103. B
104. C
105. B
106. A
107. A
108. A
109. E
110. A
111. D
112. A
113. E
114. C
115. B
116. A
117. E
118. B
119. B
120. C
121. A
122. D
123. D
124. B
125. B
126. D
127. C
128. E
129. D
130. C
131. D
132. D
133. A
134. D
135. E
136. D
137. C
138. B
139. E
140. B
141. E
142. B
143. D
144. E
145. B
146. B
147. E
148. C
149. B
150. A
151. C
152. A
153. B
154. C
155. D
156. C
157. E
158. D
159. A
160. B
161. C
162. B
163. E
164. C
165. A
166. A
167. B
168. C
169. C
170. A
171. A
172. E
173. A
174. E
175. A
176. D
177. B
178. B
179. D
180. C
181. B
182. D
183. D
184. A
185. C
186. B
187. A
188. D
189. A
190. E
191. D
192. D
193. D
194. E
195. D
196. A
197. C
198. A
199. E
200. B

EXPLANATORY ANSWERS

SAMPLE TEST 3

1. (E) According to several learning theorists (Hull, Spence, Miller, to name just a few) learning will occur in so far as the animal can obtain a goal which will lead to the reduction of a drive. A goal merely refers to that place or state where some need or motive can be satisfied.

2. (D) Absolute threshold is a psychophysical term. It refers to the least amount of energy which can be registered by a sense organ. It should be distinguished from difference thresholds, which refer to the difference between two stimuli which is necessary for the subject to judge the stimuli as different.

3. (C) Avoidance learning refers to a process in which the animal is confronted with an aversive stimulus which can be avoided if he learns to do something, such as pressing a lever. It should be distinguished from escape learning, where the animal <u>must</u> experience the aversive stimulus, but, by learning, he can escape it after a very brief interval of exposure.

4. (B) Ethnocentrism is a social psychological concept developed by Levinson; it is measured by the "E" Scale. The concept arose out of the work of Adorno and Frenkel-Brunswik on the authoritarian personality. Their theorizing attempts to find psychoanalytic bases for prejudice.

5. (A) Osgood's Semantic Differential technique is an attempt to measure meaning by measuring where a word is placed along different semantic coordinates. The key dimensions which distinguish semantic meanings are good-bad, active-passive and strong-weak (evaluative, activity and potency, respectively).

6. (A) The unconditioned stimulus elicits a response (the unconditioned response) before conditioning has occurred. After it is repeatedly paired with some previously neutral stimulus (the conditioned stimulus), this latter stimulus will elicit a response similar to the unconditioned response by itself.

7. (D) Deviation ratio is not used to measure variability. We should note the standard deviation is the most frequently used estimate of variability; the standard deviation equals the square root of the variance.

8. (D) Freud had postulated that the death wish occurs because of man's need to return to a state of quiescence. This notion is not accepted today; psychologists have found no evidence to support the idea of a death wish in man.

9. (E) The Luchins test was originally employed to measure "rigidity" in the personality. It requires the ability to shift "set" between items on the test. In other words, a good score will reflect flexibility or no fixed mental set.

10. (D) Skinner has defined a reinforcer as anything which will strengthen a stimulus-response connection when presented just after the correct response. A reinforcer need not be a drive reducer; it need just facilitate learning in the Skinnerian sense.

11. (E) Drive reduction theory holds that no learning can take place unless the learning serves to alleviate some need. In its strong form, drive reduction theory states that alleviation of needs is both necessary and sufficient for learning to occur; in its weaker form, it states that alleviation of need is sufficient for learning to occur.

12. (A) By definition, reaching a goal will be satisfying some motive. We should note that at the goal, the organism may be making consummatory responses; for example, a hungry rat reaches the goal, the place where food is. At the goal, he will make the consummatory response of eating.

13. (B) This study points out that soft textures are very important to young organisms. Harlow's monkeys showed more positive response in the presence of a soft cloth monkey that did not give milk than a wire monkey which did give milk.

14. (A) Money is a goal which obviously does not satisfy any of the primary biological needs. Money is used as a means to satisfy other needs; it is therefore called a secondary goal.

15. (B) Evidence that deprivation of a drive causes it to dominate behavior is substantial. For example, food-deprived humans were able to report thinking only about food after a lengthy period of deprivation. We should note that in psychoanalytic theory, it is assumed that inability to fulfill sexual drives leads into turning them into higher cultural drives (sublimation).

16. (D) "Directiveness" in therapy refers to how much the psychoanalyst will actually tell the patient what to do. In the client-centered therapy of Carl Rogers, there is little directiveness, and so the therapy is classified as non-directive.

17. (A) Repression refers to the burying of a painful idea or memory out of the reach of the subconscious mind. The other defense mechanisms: projection, rationalization, reaction formation, etc. are all means of dealing with some repressed idea.

18. (E) When one desires to do very well and does only moderately well, he feels that he has failed. One judges a performance in terms of one's expectations or aspirations of it. Level of aspiration can also be influenced by how well the rest of the group is doing.

19. (A) Since we plot number of trials on the abscissa, the curve will go from left to right; since errors decrease as more trials are performed, the curve will decrease from left to right.

20. (D) Spontaneous recovery will occur in both classical and operant conditioning procedures after extinction. It suggests that the phenomenon of extinction has to do with a suppression of the conditioned response, and not a complete abolition of it.

21. (E) A plateau is a flat part of a learning curve where no improvement is shown. After the plateau, learning will again be shown.

22. (D) Recall requires the subject to provide all the information that he knows. Multiple-choice tests would be an example of recognition: the student must recognize which is the correct response from among the different alternatives.

23. (D) In habituation and desensitization, we try to make the animal as familiar as we can with the environment, so that he will not respond to it. In extinction, the animal receives no reinforcement, and learns not to respond to the conditioned stimuli. Therefore, habituation, desensitization and extinction are all correct.

24. (C) Serial learning refers to the learning of items in a series. It is a technique used to study the skill of rote memorization. Serial learning is easier than paired associates learning since, in serial learning, each item serves both as a response to the previous one and as a stimulus for the following one.

25. (B) Transference in analysis refers to the patient's attaching his feelings about significant others in his life to the psychoanalyst. If the feelings

attached are those of hostility, etc., the the transference is called negative.

26. (C) We recognize that there are many different types of anxiety possible; anxiety can exist because of repression, because of fear of bodily harm, or because of fear of failure. All anxieties are characterized by a manifest state of general uneasiness; hence, this is the most inclusive definition.

27. (C) If we can recognize that particular meaning of any given situation as distinct from other situations, it is likely that we will know which situations are threatening and which are not. Fear will then be appropriately situation specific, and not generalized.

28. (E) In a conflict situation, there is a tendency to approach and a tendency to avoid. The approach tendency is stronger farther away from the goal, but since the avoidance gradient is steeper than the approach gradient, the approach gradient will be lesser than the avoidance gradient near the goal. At the point where the approach and avoidance gradients meet, there will be maximum conflict. This conflict theory is attributed to the work of Neal Miller.

29. (C) The Young-Helmholtz theory is a parsimonious theory, depending on three colors only. Recently, Hurvich and Jameson have proposed a theory similar to that of Hering, based on contrasting color pairs.

30. (E) When we rationalize, we know that there is good reason not to do something that we want to do. We will look for excuses to do this, to give us a reason for the action, so that we can ignore those reasons indicating that the action is not good.

31. (C) Much of our behavior occurs in the absence of direct physiological motivation. (For example, there is no direct physiological motive for seeking money.) Concepts are needed to explain behavior which occurs in the absence of primary needs: both functional autonomy and secondary drive are such concepts.

32. (C) A photochemical event involves a chemical reactions initiated by light, as in a photographic film and on the retina.

33. (D) The rods are rod-like retinal structures which contain visual purple (needed for dark vision) and mediate black and white vision. In the dark we want to focus where there is the most visual purple; hence, we focus where the rods are most dense.

34. (C) An illusion refers to a perception which is considered as mistaken because it does not agree with some other experience, such as objective measurement, which is taken as more fundamental.

35. (E) Reaction formation is a defense mechanism in which a subject denies a disapproved motive (hostility to the child) by giving strong expressing to the opposite (affection to the child).

36. (D) Anorexia is a neurological condition which leads to loss of appetite. It may originate in the hypothalamus.

37. (D) This study suggests that there is some innate homeostatic mechanism in the body which causes the organism to seek balanced diet without teaching.

38. (B) The use of a concrete illustration in teaching an abstract concept is known as the case-study method. Giving an example enables the subject to translate the abstraction into meaningful, everyday terms, and so better understand the underlying abstraction.

39. (A) Pitch is a qualitative dimension of hearing correlated with the frequency of the sound waves that constitute the stimulus. Higher frequencies yield higher pitches.

40. (A) Extensional meaning refers to the public meanings of something; the meaning can be conveyed by pointing to the relevant objects or events in the environment.

41. (C) The previous habit will cause proactive inhibition, and hinder the

learning of new habits appropriate to solving the new problems.

42. (A) Imprinting refers to an innate (unlearned) response, in which ducks and geese will follow whatever they are exposed to during a certain critical period in early life. Hess has found that the critical period is from 13 to 16 hours after birth in ducklings.

43. (E) Adaptive behavior will bring the organism into adjustment with its environment. If the belt were made even tighter, the man would be conscious of it at first, but would then adapt on this new level.

44. (E) Distress and delight become apparent at 3 months of age. By one year of age, distress has been differentiated into fear, disgust, anger and distress; delight has been differentiated into elation, affection, and delight.

45. (C) Gesell has compiled extensive schedules of maturation by human infants; the average infant can sit at age of 7 months, although development is not identical for all infants.

46. (C) Because there is no correlation between sensori-motor development intelligence, early intelligence tests (before 18 months) which measure sensorimotor abilities will have virtually no correlation with adult intelligence.

47. (E) The phi phenomenon is a form of stroboscopic motion. It is commonly produced by turning on and off two separated stationary light sources; as the first is turned off and the second turned on, the subject will perceive that light is moving from the position of the first to the second.

48. (A) The Stanford-Binet has been revised with a mean of 100 and a standard deviation of 16. A score of 132 is thus 2 standard deviations above the mean.

49. (E) Mongolianism is a form of mental retardation which seems to come from disturbed metabolism originating in glandular defects. This disorder occurs most frequently among children born late in the mother's reproductive life. It is possible that a mother nearing the menopause may provide an inadequate pre-natal environment for the offspring.

50. (C) Most forms of severe retardation are not known to be hereditary; hence, parents of average ability may often produce a child with severe mental retardation.

51. (A) Several schools of psychology stress the importance of understanding in learning. Theorists of these schools believe that although simple habits and associations may be formed, they are not an adequate explanation of the various phenomena of human behavior. Phenomenologists, dissonance theorists and Gestalt theorists all belong to this class of psychologist.

52. (A) Closure is a concept of Gestalt psychology. Gestaltists emphasized the idea that perception will occur in terms of the total configuration; total configuration is more satisfying. Hence, there exists a tendency toward closure.

53. (D) The name psychophysics was coined by Fechner to refer to the study of the relationship between mental processes and the physical world (sensations and physical stimuli). It is now usually restricted to the study of the sensory consequences of controlled physical stimulation.

54. (B) The arithmetic mean, mode, median, and geometric mean are measures of central tendency. The arithmetic mean is the sum of a group of observations divided by number of observations. The mode is the most frequently recurring value. The median divides the total observations into two halves. The geometric mean is the nth root of the product (of "N" observations $\{G = \sqrt[n]{x_1 x_2 \ldots x_n}\}$). The range is a measure of dispersion or variation.

55. (E) Affective disorders include manic-depressive reaction and psychotic depressive reaction. They are classed as functional psychoses: that is, disorders of psychological origin without clearly defined cause of structural change.

56. (B) Schizophrenic symptoms are greatly varied; there are 9 subclasses of the condition. Very often, the patient withdraws from reality completely into a world of his own. Schizophrenic behavior is always ill-organized; there are often profound differences between emotion and conduct.

57. (A) An hysterial sympton will occur when there are no organic or emotional bases for the behavior. A person with normal limbs may become unable to walk, or a person with normal eyes will be unable to see. Hysterical symptoms do not refer to overly emotional behavior which is appropriate to the situation.

58. (B) The sum of the deviations about the arithmetic mean is equal to zero. The following illustration exemplified the problem.

Observations	Mean $(\overline{X})$	Deviation from Mean $(X - \overline{X})$
3	6	-3
7	6	+1
9	6	+3
10	6	+4
1	6	-5
6	6	0
$\Sigma X = 36$		$\Sigma(X - \overline{X}) = 0$

$$\text{Mean} = \frac{\Sigma X}{n} = \frac{36}{n} = 6$$

59. (C) Although the polygraph is referred to as a lie detector, it operates by measuring heart rate, respiration rate and perspiration rate simultaneously.

60. (E) Analysis of variance is used to compare scores among many groups subject to different experimental conditions. It can be used only if the data are interval (if there are equal distances between the scale units of the measuring instrument). Analysis of variance would be used to compare scores of the 6 groups in the experiment.

61. (E) Stratified random sampling means that first, we select for our sample similar strata as exist in the population at large. That is, if the population is 70% middle class and 30% lower class, we would select middle and lower class subjects; those used in the final sample would be selected randomly within the lower class and within the middle class, so that 70% of the sample would be randomly selected middle class subjects, and 30% would be randomly selected lower class subjects.

62. (A) Statistical regression refers to the fact that extreme members of the population will tend to regress toward the mean . Very tall fathers are thus also likely to have somewhat shorter sons. In psychological testing, regression will occur so that extreme scores will tend to move toward the mean on retesting.

63. (E) A longitudinal study will deal with the behavior of the same subjects at different times in their lives. It should be distinguished from a cross-sectional study: here, we study two-year-olds and five-year-olds, but different ones at the same time. In a longitudinal study, we wait for the two-year-olds to become five years old in order to study their behavior.

64. (C) Von Frisch's study is interesting in that it showed that an elaborate communication system exists among bees. The form of the communication is a "dance."

65. (D) "Distribution" may be defined as the manner in which observations are spaced or located on a measurement scale. "Epidemic" may be defined as "a sudden increase in the prevalence of a disease which is more or less constantly present." "Incidence" may be defined as "the rate at which a disease or other condition develops."

66. (D) Attitudes are considered a function of a particular environment; it is reasonable that changes in both physical and psychological environment will produce changes in attitudes, making them less stable than values and vocational interests.

67. (D) The fact that subjects cannot exist for any great length of time in a sensory deprivation situation indicates that man has a strong need for stimulus input.

68. (D) Pecking order is an example of a dominance hierarchy; this is a social situation with clearly defined status roles, so that one organism dominates all below it, and so on down to the organisms dominated by all.

69. (C) Adaptation refers to adjustment. Sensory adaptation involves a change in the characteristics of experience as a result of prior stimulation, as when we see something more clearly in a darkened room, or taste something as especially sour after eating sweets.

70. (D) Eidetic imagery is imagery of such clarity that the objects represented appear to be, in some respects, present. It is similar to hallucinations, but believed to be normal in many children at early age levels.

71. (B) In normal children, the left hemisphere specializes in linguistic functions; the right, in spatial processing. In dyslexics, however, both hemispheres seem to be involved in spatial, holistic processing, causing a deficit in linguistic, sequential cognitive processing.

72. (E) The operation's aim is to help the patient adjust better with his environment.

73. (B) The second paragraph describes the work of Dr. Walter R. Hess and his experiments with electrodes implanted in a cat's brain. The last sentence of that paragraph summarizes that Dr. Hess was able to determine how parts of the brain control organs of the body.

74. (A) Your degree of visual acuity is measured by how small a separation in a ring you can see at a specified distance and with a specified intensity of illumination. The ability to observe a small separation of objects on the retina depends on the lens and refractive media of your eye, but it also depends on the separation of receptive fields in the retina. This is the Landolt ring test.

75. (D) The senses are usually defined as the higher senses of hearing and vision, and the lower (because they mediate a less rich variety of experience) senses of smell, taste, and the skin senses (touch, pain, warmth and cold).

76. (A) Extinction refers to the dropping of a response from the behavioral repertory of the organism. A learned response will extinguish in the absence of reinforcement. Since the response may show "spontaneous recovery" after a rest period, we assume that extinction does not involve complete unlearning or eradication of the response.

77. (B) Self-approval for a correct response means that the individual receives reinforcement for answering correctly despite any external reaction. Doing well pleases him; he will continue to do well no matter what the external condition he finds himself in (presence or absence of authority figures, etc.).

78. (C) Skinnerian theory holds that a reinforcement following a response will strengthen a stimulus-response connection. For this reason, it is important to know exactly what response is being reinforced, so that we can control the associations that are being learned.

79. (A) The median is the middle score of data ordered from the lowest to the highest; it is the exact middle in the sense of a center line of a highway.

80. (D) In order for conditioning to occur, the conditioned response must occur without the presentation of the unconditioned stimulus; that is, the conditioned response must follow directly on the presentation of the conditioned stimulus.

81. (E) Instinct is a descriptive term for a complex unlearned adaptive process. It may be an unlearned pattern of reflexes, also. If the adjustment were learned, it would then be called a habit. Most human behavior is learned, and so instinct can describe but a small portion of it.

82. (B) Homeostasis is the compensatory mechanism whereby a constant state is maintained. This can be physiological, it would be exemplified by sweating or

other bodily processes which maintain a constant temperature when the external temperature is too high.

83. (A) The median, mode and mean in a normal distribution are at the same point; the distribution of scores fall and become a normal curve. These measures of central tendency fall at different points when the distribution is skewed.

84. (B) The trend line Y = 1.02x represents a straight line with a slope of .02 and a Y intercept (it crosses the Y axis) at the origin.

85. (A) The correlation coefficient ranges from -1 to +1.00. A -1.00 correlation coefficient indicates a perfect indirect relationship, while a +1.00 correlation coefficient indicates a perfect direct relationship.

86. (B) When the self realistically mirrors the experience of the organism, the person is said to be mature and functioning well. Incongruence, on the other hand, between the self and the organism, or between actual experience and the ideal self, causes anxiety in the person.

87. (A) Gough's CPI is an attempt to measure personality by measuring the stable social traits in the personality; it differs from the MMPI which tries to assess pathology in the personality.

88. (B) Psychosis has been shown to be more prevalent in the lower than in the upper classes, while neurosis is more prevalent among the upper classes, according to the Hollingshead and Redlich study of prevalence and incidence of mental illnesses.

89. (D) Alcoholics Anonymous seems to provide social support--the sense of community with people in a similar plight--to the alcoholic. He is better able to work out appropriate responses to his new situation in the company of others like himself. He receives constant reinforcement from the others in the group for staying away from alcohol; no other form of therapy can provide this constant reinforcement.

90. (A) In group therapy, the patient discusses his problems with others and with the psychiatrist or counselor, all of whom meet in a group. Transference refers to attaching the feelings one has toward significant others in one's life onto the therapist; here, the feelings are transferred to the group as a whole, or, in other words, to all the members of the group.

91. (A) Schachter's work on "Communication, Deviation and Rejection" has indicated that any person whose opinions deviate far from those of the group will be rejected by the group, communication to the deviate will cease.

92. (C) Berlyne is noted for his experiments in esthetics and the esthetic value of different perceptual patterns. The conclusions of this research indicate that those patterns judged most pleasant are somewhat predictable, and the elements composing the pattern are familiar.

93. (E) In the Asch experiments, stooges agree on an answer which has objectively very little credibility. The situation is used to study conformity behavior on the part of the "real" subject.

94. (A) If a fear appeal creates strong anxieties in a subject, he may "turn off" and not comprehend the appeal, so that he will show no opinion change. If the appeal is totally reassuring, the subject will not get aroused enough to pay attention to the communication and will not show opinion change.

95. (D) Research has not proven the effectiveness of "subliminal" appeals, whether these appeals have been presented by film or television media.

96. (C) Descriptive statistics include any kind of data processing (such as development of tables, graphs, and charts) which does not attempt to infer anything that goes beyond the data themselves. Inferential or inductive statistics is the use of statistics to make generalizations about the population from observations made on samples.

97. (E) All of the listed tests are statistical tests of probability (p). They are tests of the probability of a difference as great as an observed difference or greater than an observed difference occurring by chance.

98. (C) Incidental learning is referred to as passive learning; it is learning which occurs without trying, in the absence of incentives or rewards.

99. (B) Monocular cues require one eye only; they are contrasted with binocular cues, requiring both eyes. Binocular cues are instrumental in depth perception.

100. (B) Signal detection is concerned with the subject's judgement, problems of attention, such as vigilance associated with radar tracking.

101. (E) The principle of contiguity is clearly exemplified in classical conditioning. The conditioned stimulus must be contiguous with the unconditioned stimulus in order for conditioning to occur.

102. (D) The measures of the dependent variable in instrumental conditioning are most frequently rate of response and cumulative response over time; Skinner typically measured cumulative responses over time.

103. (B) Non-parametric statistics were devised to handle data which does not come from a normally distributed population, or from an interval scale. In other words, non-parametric statistics do not require rigid or strict assumptions about the nature of the data.

104. (C) Learning can show a decrement owing to many causes. The learned response may not be reinforced, and so it will extinguish. External stimuli may serve to inhibit the learned response. After a long period of massed practice, fatigue may set in and cause a decrement in performance.

105. (B) Human engineering (or human factors research) is an applied science, participated in jointly by engineers and psychologists, concerned with the design of equipment and the arrangement of work conditions to provide the most effective combination of man and machine.

106. (A) Content analysis breaks down and categorizes the contents of a body of literature or advertising. Literature can thus be categorized as more or less propagandistic, according to an a priori scheme of analysis.

107. (A) The psychoneurotic reactions are best considered as learned reactions to stress and frustration. Neuroses include anxiety reaction, conversion reaction, phobic reaction and obsessive-compulsive reaction. The disturbance is not so severe as to produce a profound personality derangement, as in the psychoses.

108. (A) Functional psychoses should be distinguished from organic psychoses. Functional psychosis is defined as a psychotic disorder of psychological origin that has no clearly defined structural changes.

109. (E) Hebephrenic behavior is one of the four most common forms of schizophrenia; it is characterized by childish and regressed behavior; the typical hebephrenic will talk a babble referred to as "word salad." Other common forms of the disease are paranoid, catatonic, and simple schizophrenia.

110. (A) Hypomania can be a phase of manic-depressive psychosis; it is characterized by extreme excitement on the part of the patient. Hypomania is controlled through the use of tranquilizers.

111. (D) It should be obvious that when we have conflicting motives, performance of one action will satisfy one motive and leave the other unsatisfied; the individual will be in a state of frustration. Frustration in animals has been studied in the laboratory largely by blocking goals.

112. (A) The general adaptation syndrome is Selye's term for the typical sequence of events when the body is subjected to severe stress, moving from the alarm reaction through resistance, to exhaustion.

113. (E) The hypothalamus is one of the structures at the base of the brain which is significant in sleep, and in emotional and motivational behavior. We should note that the adrenal medulla (part of the adrenal gland, and not the brain) is also significant in emotional behavior.

114. (C) Fixation has been demonstrated experimentally by Maier, in frustrated rats. They keep performing the same unsuccessful action repeatedly. The term is also used in psychoanalysis: it refers to arrested development due to failure to pass beyond one of the earlier stages of psychosexual development.

115. (B) In order for a term to be useful psychologically, we must be able to provide it with an operational definition. Meaning as defined as part of a response elicited by a stimulus provides us with an adequate operational definition of meaning.

116. (A) Nonsense words are defined as "nonsense" just because they do not resemble in statistical terms the properties of non-nonsense English syllables. It has been found that words with meaning are more easily learned than pure nonsense syllables.

117. (E) Incubation is the second of four stages in creative thought proposed by Wallas; the states are: preparation, incubation, illumination, and verification. In incubation, the preparation leads to creative thought by means of a process we do not fully understand as yet.

118. (B) We develop a mental set (or method of approach) to successive problems of the same general type. This is called "learning to learn."

119. (B) The serial position effect refers to the process in which we learn the first and last parts of a list (or poem) better than the middle part. To compensate for this, more effort should be devoted to studying the middle part.

120. (C) The teacher would correctly offer the student partial (or intermittent) reinforcement by praising him for a good contribution to class discussion. Research has shown that learning based on partial reinforcement is most resistant to extinction.

121. (A) Formal discipline is an older interpretation of transfer of training, justifying the study of a subject not for its own sake, but for the training it supposedly gives the mental faculties.

122. (D) F. S. Werblin, "The Control of Sensitivity in the Retina," <u>Scientific American</u> (January 1973) 71 gives a full discussion of this question.

123. (D) Skinner is primarily an empiricist; he believes that we must gather data and observe the lawful relationships between stimuli and responses before we start forming theories about them.

124. (B) The first occurrence of an operant behavior is theoretically inexplicable; even Skinner cannot pinpoint why it occurs. The reason is that an operant behavior is <u>not</u> a response to a clearly defined external stimulus.

125. (B) The ego-ideal refers to who we feel, as children, that our parents would most like to be; the role model is some person that one patterns oneself on.

126. (D) Freud held that development takes place through five psychosexual stages (oral, anal, phallic, latent, genital). Each stage is characterized by a zone of pleasurable stimulation and appropriate objects of sexual attachment, culminating in normal heterosexual mating.

127. (C) According to Freud, we can, in dreams, obtain the fulfillment of wishes that either cannot be expressed, or are frustrated in attainment, in the waking state.

128. (E) "The number of degrees of freedom is always equal to the number of observations minus the number of necessary relations obtaining among these observations." (H. M. Walker, "Degrees of Freedom," <u>Journal of Educational Psychology</u>, 1940, 31:253-269.) The number of degrees of freedom characterizing the data indicated in the question cannot be determined from the information given because we are

not told how many necessary relations are involved.

129. (D) A perfect negative correlation would exist between a given rank order and its inverse. The correlation co-efficient of a perfect negative correlation would be -1.

130. (C) Recent research on the skin sense has shown that under certain conditions, a hot object will produce the sensation of cold; this is referred to as "paradoxical" cold.

131. (D) The Purkinje phenomenon is a shift in relative brightness value as illumination changes, such as the greater relative brightness of yellow in daylight and of blue in twilight illumination.

132. (D) The person with normal color vision will be able to perceive all colors from a mixture of the three primaries; the most normal form of color blindness involves the ability to differentiate only two primaries. Protonopes lack sensitivity to the red end of the spectrum, and deuteronopes lack sensitivity to the blue-green end.

133. (A) These experiments indicate that there is some physiological need for dreaming, not just a psychological need. It is possible (but not proven as yet) that important biochemical changes occur during dreaming.

134. (D) Experimental evidence has shown that a period of learning, followed by a period of sleep and then testing, yields the best test results. It is based on the "consolidation" theory, which assumes that in the absence of external stimulation (sleep), the material learned will consolidate.

135. (E) Individual curves show us the development of single persons and enable us to compare people. Average curves do not allow for such comparisons; we can get only trends of development from average curves.

136. (D) Vectors are a term used in Kurt Lewin's theories; they refer to the forces (or pulls) acting on an individual or a group toward different actions.

137. (C) Gestalt psychology is concerned with configurations; in other words, the totality of a perception. If different aspects of the perceptual field are changed, perception will be altered; i.e., a figure will be perceived differently when placed in different figure-ground relationships.

138. (B) Retroactive inhibition will impinge on a memory trace and cause the trace to be forgotten. In the same way, negative transfer will hinder the task to be learned. Negative transfer will occur, for example, when we must make different responses to very similar stimuli.

139. (E) Many behaviors will not appear until the organism has matured sufficiently for the function to emerge, no matter how much previous practice there has been. However, once the organism is mature enough, practice will improve performance of the particular function.

140. (B) Co-twin control uses identical twins; in this way, the psychologist hopes to control the effects of heredity, while varying the effects of environment systematically.

141. (E) Proactive inhibition is said to occur when the learning of one habit interferes with the learning or retention of a subsequent habit. Retroactive inhibition refers to the forgetting of a first habit as a result of the learning of the second one.

142. (B) In order to test for retroactive inhibition, we must see whether the learning of a second task has a detrimental effect on the first one. If we are interested in the retroactive inhibition of task A by task B, we must use the design in which A, then B, then A are performed; we can compare the A scores before and after B, and if the scores worsen from before to after, we can say that retroactive inhibition has occurred.

143. (D) A succinct account of the super-

ego is given by Hall and Lindzey in "Psychoanalytic Theory and its Applications in the Social Sciences" in Lindzey (ed.), Handbook of Social Psychology. George Herbert Mead has elaborated his idea of the "generalized other" in various places, including his Mind, Self and Society (Chicago, University of Chicago Press, 1934). The psychoanalytic threefold division of Ego, Id, and Superego finds something of a parallel in Mead's notions of "I," "Me," and "Generalized Other."

144. (E) Aphasia is an organically caused speech impairment. Hysteria, amnesia, dissociative reaction and fugue refer to different varieties of a psychoneurotic disorder classified under the general term dissociation.

145. (B) Dissonance theory is a social psychological theory which accounts for post-decisional behaviors. Resonance theory, frequency theory, volleyplace theory and Von Bekesy's theory are all theoretical explanations of auditory phenomena.

146. (B) Autobiographical statements and vocational interest questionnaires will most likely correlate well with the desired criteria. The other measures are largely personality tests, and will not correlate with the vocational criteria needed.

147. (E) Biserial correlation is the statistical technique used to determine the relationship between two measures when one is a scale on a continuum (here, the test performance) and the other is some dichotomous classification (here, staying with the company vs. not staying with the company).

148. (C) In the critical period, there is maximal possibility for imprinting; the organism will follow the "mother object" and the organism's social behavior will be influenced by this consequent behavior.

149. (B) Imprinting behavior is more influenced by what the organism first imprinted on; discrimination learning is more influenced by the most recent stimulus presented.

150. (A) Fear increases, and so later imprinting becomes more difficult, according to Hess.

151. (C) The y variable increases and then decreases as x increases.

152. (A) See any standard psychology text chapter on psychophysics.

153. (B) The psychological theorist is most interested in the particular kind of stimuli that can be used to motivate learning. Therefore, the information that the conditioned stimulus of the white box acquires negative incentive properties and motivates the rat to learn to escape is of the greatest interest.

154. (C) Classical conditioning will occur when a previously neutral stimulus is paired in time with some unconditioned stimulus--in this case, the aversive stimulus of the shock. The rat responds to the white box (the previously neutral, or conditioned stimulus) just as he did to the shock; classical conditioning has occurred. In the second part of the experiment, the rat shows instrumental conditioning: his learned responses to the white box are instrumental in enabling him to escape.

155. (D) A negative correlation occurs when a high score on one scale is correlated with a low score on another scale. The negative correlation between neurotic tendency and self-sufficiency is the same as the correlation between self-sufficiency and neurotic tendency. Filling in the other half of the matrix would just duplicate the information we already have.

156. (C) The correlation between A and B is the same as the correlation between B and A. In other words, the correlation between neurotic tendency and self-sufficiency is the same as the correlation between self-sufficiency and neurotic tendency. Filling in the other half of the matrix would just duplicate the information we already have.

157. (E) The limit on validity is approximately the square root of the reliability. Therefore, since .90 is approximately the square root of .80, it would be the limit of validity.

158. (D) In its later form, the Law of Effect states that a stimulus-response connection can be strengthened by a reward that follows it.

159. (A) Reward will reinforce the organism for a specific response. Punishment will tell him "Stop that!" but will not tell him the correct response; it therefore does not convey much information.

160. (B) Alternative B indicates a strong tendency for the subject to repeat a response without reward or punishment; this alternative is damaging to Thorndike's position.

161. (C) In order for punishment to be effective, the organism must not only know that he has done something wrong; he must know what he should be doing; therefore, it is important that punishment occur when the correct response is immediately accessible.

162. (B) The author is interested in those measurements which will give us information in terms of the totality that we are studying. Observer rating scales would describe the activity of the group as a whole, and thus be the most "molar" tool.

163. (E) Gestalt theorists are interested in the total configuration; their approach is thus also a wholist, or molar one.

164. (C) These stages are related to Freud's belief that sexual instincts did not appear suddenly at puberty, but were elaborated through a course of development beginning in earliest infancy, a course of development involving a sequence of errogenous zones. The first zone in this sequence was the mouth (oral stage), the second was the anus, and the third was the genital, to which the term phallic was also given.

165. (A) Cf. Otto Klineberg, "Tests of Negro Intelligence," in: Otto Klineberg (ed), Characteristics of the American Negro (N. Y., Harper, 1944).

166. (A) The classic study of this subject is T. W. Adarno et al, The Authoritarian Personality (N. Y., Harper, 1950).

167. (B) There is a definite tendency for x and y to be associated.

168. (C) It must be recognized that these are 2 x 2 tables of association. In table #1 the missing cell entries can be computed because the row and column marginals are equal, thereby providing a basis for computations.

169. (C) The fourth cell of table #3 would be the sum of the fourth cells of tables #1 and #2.

170. (A) The frustration-aggression hypothesis holds that all frustration will lead to aggressive behavior. The frustrated rat here is aggressive to both another rat and to the doll, presumably because he is frustrated. The frustration-aggression hypothesis was created by Miller.

171. (A) Stimulus generalization refers to making the same response to a new stimulus as to the old one when the new one is perceived as similar or equivalent to the old one. It is important to note that in stimulus generalization, the response to old and new stimuli is similar.

172. (E) Displacement refers to the transference of feeling from the hated object to some other object. The rat has displaced his aggression from the "bystander" rat to the doll.

173. (A) Piaget refers to adaptation as a balance between assimilation and accommodation; assimilation refers to the changes the organism makes on its environment, while accommodation refers to the way the organism is changed by its environment.

174. (E) An operation is an action which has been internalized. The child first learns to do certain actions and then is able to work out how it is going to do a typical action before acting. Thought, according to Piaget, originates in the internalization of actions.

175. (A) The affinity between Piaget's groupings of operations and Bruner's strategies (which show the patterning of adult decision processes in learning a new concept) occurs because both attempt to

model the actual structure of thought processes, fixating on what is crucial in the thought system.

176. (D) Cognitive dissonance theory is concerned with attitude change and other behaviors following a decision; these behaviors should enable consistency for the subject. Here, subjects had to lie; after the lie, if the subject were paid $20, he believed he lied for this money, but if he were just paid $1, he lied for no good reason, so he reduced his dissonance and believed the lie.

177. (B) If the subjects had been required to tell the lie, they would say that they had not done it of their own will and would have no need to rationalize their behavior; in other words, they would believe the experimenter, not themselves, had lied. Dissonance thus cannot be produced unless the dissonance-producing act is performed by the subject of his own volition.

178. (B) The dependent variable is what the psychologist measures; here, he measured the extent to which the subject believed the lie.

179. (D) Factor analysis attempts to see exactly what a test is measuring, and thus, how related tests which purport to measure the same thing are. Thus, alternatives A, B, and C are all true.

180. (C) Simple structure is designed to give an efficient explanation of what the test measures; it is therefore best met when each test can be described in terms of a few factors.

181. (B) Factor analysis attempts to discover the meaning of a test by discovering and exploring its correlations with other variables. A "factor loading" will demonstrate which of the tests are tapping which of the factors. If a test loads high on a factor, it measures that factor, and if it does not load high, there is no relation between the factor and the test.

182. (D) This is the group not subjected to the experimental variation. Changes between X_1 and X_2 can be compared with changes between Y_1 and Y_2 , with any differences being presumably the result of the experimental variation. Group Y is thus said to be a "control" group, against whom the X group can be checked at Time 2.

183. (D) As an ex post facto study it would be limited to Time 2. As a study of alcoholics, it would necessarily involve the examination of group X (i.e., those who have undergone the process of becoming alcoholics).

184. (A) L. L. Thurstone was one of the pioneers of factor analysis in this country. He does not believe in the existence of general factors, as does the English factor analyst, Spearman.

185. (C) The dependent variable refers to what the psychologist measures. In this instance, the reporting of the presentation of the word by the observer is the dependent variable.

186. (B) The hungry subjects would be more motivated towards food; they would be able to see food at a lower recognition threshold than would sated subjects.

187. (A) Later experiments which controlled frequency of occurrence in dirty and non-dirty words did not find the perceptual defense phenomena to occur.

188. (D) Determinism would have everything about the organism fixed from birth or early childhood; the view stated here holds that man is constantly changing as a result of beliefs about the future.

189. (A) Adler holds that man will make his own personality; with greater creativity, the personality will be more nearly perfect. He holds that we are responsible for our own personalities.

190. (E) Krech is a social psychologist, who has done work with the effects of early environment on the neural development of rats, but not in nerve recording. The physiological psychologist Mueller is known for his research in nerve recording.

191. (D) Festinger is associated with social psychology, in particular, with

group behavior, social comparison theory and dissonance theory, not with psychometrics.

192. (D) Bales is a social psychologist who is known for work in group process and the development of group observation techniques.

193. (D) Fighting, fleeing, feeding and reproductive behavior--and the emotions associated with each of these acts--are characteristic of the type of emotional behavior and motivational drives thought to be dominant in the limbic system. One could make a good case for choosing choice E, the amygdala, as the correct answer, since it is believed to be strongly involved in aggressive behavior; but, the question specifically asked for a functional, not an anatomical structure.

194. (E) Different writers have drawn up different lists of ego-defense mechanisms, but options A, B, C, and D are among those most frequently included. "Alienation" is used by different writers in somewhat different ways, but for phenomena distinct from psychological defense mechanisms as commonly understood.

195. (D) The new car owners did not read ads for other types of cars, showing that they were seeking consonant information after their decision; the greater the number of cars they had considered, the greater was their tendency to seek consonant information, showing that increasing the number of alternatives increases dissonance.

196. (A) Conflict theory attempts to determine how we resolve inconsistencies in order to make a decision; dissonance theory attempts to examine post-decisional behaviors.

197. (C) Jung had a deterministic philosophy; we inherit both cultural and personal archetypes that determine our development and future behavior.

198. (A) Tests obtained below 18 months are largely sensori-motor in nature, and will not correlate with the verbal abilities tested in later life.

199. (E) A developmental study will optimally examine the behavior of the same subjects at different ages, in a longitudinal fashion. In this way, we have controlled the experiential background of the subjects, and have reduced the operation of selective factors in the study. We know that the 5-year-olds are comparable to the 2-year-olds, since they are the same subjects.

200. (B) Psychological growth curves, like learning curves, are negatively accelerated: growth is rapid at first, then slows down to reach an asymptote.